Beauty For Ashes

Make The Exchange

By Keke Hamilton

ISBN: 978-1-7378925-0-2

Cover Design: Sam

Book Design: Keke Hamilton

Editor: Erica Peter

Book Format: Pasindu Lakshan

First printing edition 2022

Dedication

This book is dedicated to all those who are searching for answers.

There's only one person who can provide them.

I pray this leads you in the right direction.

Table of Contents

Table of Contents

Introduction

For at least the past 10 years, I have lived my life with this one thought: I don't know who I will end up being when I die. But if I was in any way impactful, and they decide to do a movie on my life, I want it to show I was a good person. I don't want my movie to be filled with anger or vindictiveness. I want it to reflect goodness, and love and compassion for people and God. I want to have fulfilled God's purpose for my life. This has been at the forefront of my thoughts daily.

Most people have gone through a certain amount of hurt or pain in their lives, mostly from childhood, and they still carry that weight around today. We're all dealing with levels of trauma that we have not fully processed or even acknowledged in some cases. But in order for us to be whole and healthy, we have to do the hard work. We have to face our pain and stare it in the eye until it hurts more because digging up the past CAN and WILL be painful. You will have to be vulnerable in areas where you may have kept closed off since the trauma occurred. It's going to be necessary to unveil those parts of yourself to yourself. This pain is where you will find your healing. It takes work… HARD WORK to shed yourself of those old layers of pain that held you back from all that you were meant to be. It's so worth it though. Those layers are HEAVY! That insecurity you carry around, that self-doubt you wake up with… those things are weighing you down and you don't know how to let it go. I'm not a therapist, and I'm not pretending to be. But I was carrying around a lot of hurt and pain for a long time. And my thoughts, feelings and behavior were so destructive to myself and others. I took the time to do the work. And in doing the work to heal, I'm able to reflect back on a lot of moments. As I share some of these moments with you, I only want to help inspire you to do the same; face the hurt, then allow God to dissolve your pain.

For the longest time, I was consumed by my pain. Held prisoner by my past… and we all know hurt people, hurt people. But the main person I was hurting was myself because I wasn't aware that I was in pain. I moved through my life not loving myself or even LIKING myself! I didn't feel worthy of love from friends, family or anyone. I didn't know why I felt like this. As I got older, I began to analyze my feelings and emotions, and I understood I had been crying out for help all along. The way I allowed myself to be mistreated and abused by almost everyone in my life was a direct reflection of how I viewed myself. I went through bouts of depression, suicidal thoughts, and just plain disrespect of myself and the life that God had given me.

I tried to have conversations with the ones I felt hurt by over the years, but if my pain was never acknowledged, I could never heal, or so I thought. Healing has to be about YOU, not the other person. The truth is everyone in your life is going to hurt you. It's how you process it that counts. Most people will never acknowledge their role in your hurt or disappointment. That shouldn't stop you from moving forward and being all that God has called you to be. There is a reason for it all, even if you can't see it. God allows things to happen for your GOOD. My friend, Pastor Rich Tolbert Jr, who is also a phenomenal worship leader and top Gospel Recording Artist, once said, "God is careful to watch over His promises over your life, and God is faithful to His word." What that simply means is it's all happening for you. You're building your character for the abundance God has for you. No, it won't always feel good, but it won't defeat you. Don't wait on your healing to come from other people's validation of your pain. It's taken me YEARS to understand that. What I realized is that I had to stop looking to other people to heal me and turn to God for that. He alone healed me once I allowed Him to invade my heart. God won't force Himself on you. But if you ask Him to change you and really mean it, He will show up in the most astounding ways. He did it for me. He's waiting to do it for you.

Now, I have discovered the purpose for my pain, and hopefully, my past helps you understand a bit of yours.

Take a journey with me…

-KH

Chapter 1

In The Beginning...

I grew up on the Southside of Chicago. When people hear "Southside" or even just Chicago in general, the stereotype is that the person grew up in the projects or was poor or struggled in life. Well, that's not my story. Actually, that's a HUGE misconception! I am in my late 30s, so I grew up in a time where kids were allowed to just be kids. I lived in a middle-class neighborhood. My family consists of my parents, my two older brothers, Keith and Reggie, then me, the baby of the bunch. We lived in a community of some really sweet people who always looked out for one another. I'm talking if I was seen acting up on the block, my mama knew before I even made it home! There were a lot of kids in the neighborhood. For the most part, everyone got along. I DO remember there was a boy that lived on the street behind me that had a dog named Pepsi, and if I remember correctly, he and my brother weren't too friendly. One day, he let his dog chase me on my bike. I am still traumatized to this day! ☹ But it was a great place to live. We would block both ends of the street off and have block club parties in the summer, we'd have huge games of Hide & Seek on summer nights, and then in the winter, we'd do something REALLY fun! My block was the end of the street and there was a viaduct that cut us off from the next street. What's a viaduct? LOL (that's ok. I don't think they use that term everywhere.) A viaduct is a train track that's raised high off the ground. And because it's so high, it created a big hill. In the winters, when that hill is covered with snow, all the kids would take their sleds (we all had one) to the top and slide down the hill. BOY OH BOY!!! Those were some of my favorite memories of childhood.

I went to Summer Camp EVERY SINGLE SUMMER at Olive Harvey Community College. I had mixed feelings about the program, but I certainly looked forward to it every year. LOL! For the first half of the day, we would study reading, math, and science (I think). For the second have, we got to choose our activities. I think I did dance, some kind of sports, etc. I have NO idea now. Lol! Make no mistake, everything my parents had me in had an educational component to it, even on summer vacation. The 2 and a half months, I felt I earned the right to sleep late and NOT study. LOL! But it was a great time and I looked forward to it every year. I also went to Vacation Bible School twice a year, once at my church and once at my best friend's church. Honestly, I was in A LOT of activities all the time. Never an idle moment for us. I had a pretty good childhood growing up.

My mom was a teacher, and my dad worked at a distribution center. We also had several rental properties around the city. So being a business-minded person was instilled in me at a very early age. To top it off, we had various profitable stocks at that time. On Saturday mornings, my dad would wake us up at 7AM ☹ to check our individual stock in the newspaper, and we'd have to explain to him whether we made a profit or lost money that week. At the age I'm at now, I understand and appreciate those moments…. HOWEVER, at 11 and 12 years old, waking me up at 7am on a Saturday was NOT the move! LOL! When it came to the properties, I was right there helping out with those as well. Setting up appointments for potential tenants, keeping track of showings, helping with applications and credit check paperwork… Is it a wonder why I was never satisfied at a regular job?

Going back to my MANY extracurricular activities, writing and music have always had the most special place in my life. I started writing poems in second grade. There was a children's magazine that we used to read back then, Scholastic News. On the back, they would put the address if any child in the specified grade range wanted to submit poems. I did and guess what! I got published in the 2nd grade. So, I guess technically I've been a published author and poet since 2nd grade huh! LOL! Let me go add that to my resume real quick. BRB. ☺

I went to Amelia Earhart Elementary School. It was a small elementary school, but I loved it so much! My school went from KG-6th grade. My favorite teacher was my music teacher, Ms. Norman. She came to my school when I was in third grade. Ms. Norman was a classically trained Opera singer and literally one of the sweetest teachers I've ever met. She was young, probably in her mid 20s at the time. She was always so beautifully put together. Her perfume lingered in the room long after she was gone, and her demeanor was always poised. I honestly can't remember music classes before she got there, although I'm sure we had it. But that's how defining she was in my life. She was about to shape my love for music and being creative for the rest of my life.

My introduction of Ms. Norman was her rolling her music cart into my classroom in third grade. She introduced us to all kinds of music; different genres, different sounds. She taught us about musicals and operas, poetry and oratory speech. I was so intrigued by all of it. I myself already LOVED music. I loved to sing. So, it's safe to say I was a kid of the arts from jump. Ms. Norman had each class singing songs, learning dances and we'd perform them at various programs throughout the school year. I had been singing in the youth choir at church since I can remember, so when Ms. Norman began having us sing at school, I was so elated!! There were always solos with every song selection, and I guess she liked my voice because she chose me, Alicia, and Melissa (two of my classmates) to always sing them. KG graduation, 6th grade promotion ceremony, Black History month assembly, Christmas program… didn't matter. It was always us three. And I was honored that she chose me.

In the 3rd grade, not long after she had been there, she began choosing students to audition for the All-City Elementary Youth Choir. This was a huge, well-known choir in the city of Chicago where if your school was selected to participate, there was a certain number allowed to audition. Grades 3-8, and of those auditions, no more than 2 or 3 were chosen for the choir. Ms.

Norman chose me to audition and yep! Ya girl made it! We had rehearsal every Saturday and performed all over. Even went overseas, although my mom would not let me travel with them out of the country. Fun fact; I am going to harmonize with every single song I sing! It is so hard to sing in the key I'm listening to, even if that's the key I sing in, simply because my ears were trained to hear 4-part harmony. I can be annoying, lol, but I don't care. My friends are used to me. I love to sing still. Anyway, we would put on a HUGE show every year at Orchestral Hall in downtown Chicago. I can remember looking out into the audience and being mesmerized by the amount of people and all the lights. Tremendously nervous and frightened at the same time, but I loved every moment. After the first year, it was easier. I didn't get as nervous when that time came. I actually looked forward to it all year. What an experience!

Ms. Norman also sent me out for casting calls. Do you remember the show "The Parenthood" that Robert Townsend created? Yep! I auditioned for the role of Cici, the sassy little sister. Some of you are probably wondering why I didn't get it, as smart as MY mouth can be at times. (No one asked for your input) LOL! Well, at that time, I was just sweet and innocent. Which is why I DIDN'T get the role. I remember I was extremely nervous. I can still hear my mama say, "Just be calm and do your best baby."

I auditioned for Mr. Townsend himself. I can even remember

my audition line. It was “Call my mama now, I’m not GOING to the principal’s office.” Emphasis on “going” and with A LOT of attitude. I’d KILL that line now! LOL! But back then, not so much. I didn’t have any sass in my demeanor, but I gave it my all. When I was done saying my line, Mr. Townsend told me, “That was good. But I need Cici to have a little more attitude. Work on that and come back and audition for something else for me.” I thanked him and left. Needless to say, that was my first- and last time auditioning. LOL! I guess acting was never really my thing. It was fun though. Same with modeling. I got accepted into Modeling School my Junior year in High School, but I didn’t fully go into the program. I was EXTREMELY thin in High School. They wanted me to lose more weight. I am super glad now that I made the decision to say no on that one. That could have meant life or death for me. I’ll explain that one later. But I’ve had so many opportunities to do so many things. Choices. That’s important. And I never turned down an opportunity to give something a chance.

High School was interesting. I went to Morgan Park HS, Home of the Mustangs. THEE best school in the city of Chicago. (Go argue with someone else, this is not debatable. Lol) I was in the choir in high school as well. All 4 years. And I continued to write to help me cope with these years as well. High School. I was living in prison inside myself during these years. There were things going on… emotions all over the place. I dealt with a lot of sadness, self-hatred, depression, abandonment… you name it,

I felt it. And most people would have never known. Maybe they didn't want to see because "looking perfect" on the outside was more important than being healthy on the inside. As a result, I often crawled into my safe space and allowed the creativity to heal me. It was temporary comfort for feelings I didn't have the ability to process.

Remember how I told you I started writing poetry very early on? Welp, that never stopped. I have been writing poetry my entire life. Then I began writing songs in about 6th grade. For me, writing and singing (mostly writing) was my outlet. I felt like I could never just be myself. There were moments when I was so unsure of how I fit into the environments around me. When I felt sad, or lonely… misunderstood or unloved… I never really felt like I had anyone to talk to, so what I loved became how I expressed myself. I always felt safe in the space of creating. For me, it wasn't creating, or at least I didn't realize it back then. For me, it was a way of coping, a way of making it day-to-day. Even now, If I feel overwhelmed, I will write down how I feel. I try not to keep it bottled up because there's only so much I can keep on the inside. After a while, I will overflow with actions and behaviors that reflect all that anger and sadness.

Don't get me wrong here; I've had A LOT of angry years. That's how I can say the things I'm saying to you now. I've made tons of mistakes and bad choices. I had years of not listening to anyone because I didn't TRUST what anyone told me! NOONE!

And I was just an emotional little girl with a broken heart and no idea how to process some things I had been carrying for many years! Who do you turn to when you feel like no one is on your side? Who do you talk to when you have for your ENTIRE LIFE felt ignored and unheard? Who can you count on to validate your feelings when you have felt disregarded? Who is your savior? Who is your friend?

LITERALLY, there were years where God was my ONLY friend. And here's the thing of it, I IGNORED HIM! And that left me wandering through my life with no direction. Can you believe it?

To think that God loved me when I was careless, protected me when I was reckless, and guided me when I was senseless is enough to make me drop to my knees and worship him RIGHT NOW! You ought to open up your mouth and tell God THANK YOU right now, at this moment, for bringing you through the things you know and shielding you from the ones you don't!

What I have learned as I got older is that we ALL have trauma from our childhoods… in SOME form. Some are a lot more than others, but we are all living with things we never healed from. What I want you to remember is that life isn't always easy… in fact, OFTEN, life gets to be a bit overwhelming. You can look at someone who appears to have the sweetest childhood, adolescence and overall life. And then one day you're asking yourself what signs did you not see to know something was wrong all along. You ever just look at someone in what appears to be their "finished" stage and say, "how in the world did they survive such trauma?" Or "you hear of someone with an amazing survival story and you think "God really carried them through the storm." Well, yeah. All of that is true. You see, God ALLOWS things in our lives to happen to us because He knows we are strong enough to survive it. There is no test without a testimony. And best believe God will ALWAYS get the glory out of every situation. After all, we are only here to do His work. Just keep going forward. The rain will stop and the sun will shine. I promise. ☺

Chapter 2

Hurt People, Hurt People

You've all heard the phrase "fake it till you make it"? Well, I learned and perfected the art of faking it very early on. Those that know me today know me to be very outspoken. I am not shy at all, and I hold NOTHING back! I walk into a room of strangers and leave out with all types of connections and new "friends." That's just me! I have mastered the art of networking and I love meeting new people. It has helped provide success in various careers, including Network Marketing, and it has proven to be the way the world operates. I have worked in people-driven careers for the last 13 years, so essentially, connecting with new people has become a way of life. As the saying goes, it's not what you know but who you know. I'm not afraid to walk up to and talk to anyone and everyone about anything and everything. But it hasn't always been that way. In fact, for quite a while, it was just the opposite.

Young Keke was not a people person at heart. I always felt a little out of place. I think it was mostly because I was such a shy kid, and I was (and still am) super emotional. This left me a bit self-conscience because who wants to be the girl who cries about everything, right?! I would take every word someone said to heart. Even as a child, I would zero in on other people's hurt and it made me emotional as if it were my own emotions. I can remember getting so mad on the inside when I would start crying because I wanted to stop, but once I start, it's got to run its course. There's no controlling it. My face, lips and eyes get puffy and red, and it takes forever to clear. So yeah, there was no hiding it, and I always felt like I was on display, like there was a scarlet letter C on my forehead for crybaby.

I started Kindergarten a year earlier than kids my age. My mom enrolled me in a program where I took a test and evaluation and if I passed, I could start early. I remember testing day. I wore my favorite purple dress that made me feel strong and pretty. As my mommy held my hand walking in, I remember her saying to me, "now when we go in here, you gotta open up your mouth and talk to these people or they are not going to let you in school." I took a breath and I walked in. I was sitting across from the test moderator. Now, I don't remember the questions she asked me, but I remember the feeling. It was here that I started masking my true feelings. I was completely terrified, but at that moment, being terrified was not an option. I had to push those feelings deep down inside myself and put on a face of confidence. I answered her questions and I took my exam. I passed, so off I went to kindergarten at 4 years old. It's funny! At my age now, kindergarten still doesn't seem THAT long ago! I can remember my teacher and my friends. Some of them I'm still in contact with today! Isn't that amazing? 34 years of friendship. I'm honored to have maintained these connections.

I went to Amelia Earhart Elementary School. It was a small community elementary school on the South-east side of Chicago. Earhart went from KG-6th grade, nothing major. Very intimate. You pretty much knew the whole school. I had a pretty solid core group of friends, although I don't remember ever being at odds with anyone for real. In 3rd grade, I began singing and performing. Yes, I was still terrified, but I pushed through. I wanted to say no each and every time because of fear, but I put a smile on my face and faked my way through it. Palms sweating and all! LOL! One thing I was always determined to do was to be the best. The intense desire to please my family was so stifling at times, but not rising to the occasion was not an option. We chase love for many different reasons. Most times, we don't even realize that's what we are doing, especially when we are young. How we need to receive love never looks the same as how someone else needs to receive love. Because of this, sometimes we don't get what we need to satisfy our hearts.

My parents were amazing at providing for me and my brothers. We did not lack anything. Some may even call me spoiled. (most would call me spoiled lol) I had an overflow of things, for sure. For me, things were cool, but affection was what I craved. Please don't misunderstand me here. How we give love and how we need to receive love are sometimes different. As a parent now, I can understand this. As a child, adolescent and young adult, it made no sense. Having things were great. But I always felt misunderstood. I felt emotionally abandoned. Remember, I was a very sensitive child. Verbal validation of love, physical validation of love, and words of affirmation; these were things I wanted. That is my love language. Being able to provide a great life for your children, that is absolutely a love language as well, but for me, I needed an abundance of hugs and I love yous. Not receiving that often left me very sad with more questions than confidence.

When I was in elementary school, I began to hate the way I looked. I'm talking YOUNG… like 4th grade. I was teased by some friends and family members for being "fat," destroying my self-esteem. Being called some of the names that were said to me rang over and over in my head for most of my life. It hurt so bad being teased so hard by people I had no control over whether or not they were in my life. You can stop being friends with friends; you can't stop being family with family. My broken ego and shattered pride became a part of me for many years. Eventually, I learned to put on that face of confidence again, just so I could carry on with my day. I guess this is why I clung to music and writing the way I did. For me, it was a safe place. A place where I could shed those false faces I was forced to wear every day and just be! In middle school, I began to think about what high school would look like. I refused to go into high school as the "fat girl." Funny thing is, I was never fat to begin with. In middle school, I wore a size 8 in juniors. On what planet is that fat? And for a child? The standards that we put on ourselves and others as it relates to beauty are horrible. Anyway, I was programmed to believe I was a big girl and ugly, and I didn't want to feel that way anymore. I had to do something about it. I'd look in the mirror and absolutely HATE the image staring back at me. Everyday. All day.

I developed an eating disorder. I began vomiting up everything that went into my body. At the time, in my mind, I was in full control of it though, it was NOT in control of me. It was ALWAYS a conscious choice to throw up and I could stop at any time. Ladies listen, when your thoughts are this broken, no matter how much you think you have things under control, you don't. It's a sickness. I didn't know that then. I just wanted to lose weight. By the end of my 8th grade year, I was a size 4. I loved the way how I looked made people look at me. I'll say that again. I loved the way how I looked made people look at me. It didn't stop me from throwing up though. Why? Because when I looked in the mirror, I still saw someone overweight, although I knew I had lost a lot of weight. And on top of that, I had to maintain that size. See, even though the goal was accomplished, my mind made up reasons to justify why I could not stop. This is no different than someone addicted to drugs or alcohol. And to top it off, those very family members that teased me for being "fat" in turn began to tease me for being too skinny. The name-calling didn't end; it just shifted. This left me depressed. At 13 and 14 years old, you shouldn't be questioning whether you're too big or too small, or not pretty enough. You're just a kid and should be allowed to be one without those judgements of yourself echoing in your head. I had a very distorted image of what I looked like. All through high school, I was a size 2. I had stopped vomiting, for the most part, in my sophomore year, with the exception of the occasional purging, and that mostly was an impulse reaction to moments of feeling depressed. You see, my vomiting was a way of control in areas of my mind where I felt I had no control. Again, ladies, this is a sickness. And anyone with a friend or family member going through similar feelings, understand it's not about the weight. It's about the feelings attached to it.

I couldn't talk my feelings out with anyone. Remember, I learned from an early age to mask my fears with a smile and push through. That was what life was for me. Eventually, I became a horrible person. I had a lot of friends; we had a lot of fun… but I became a bully. I never fought anyone, but who needs to fight when you can crush someone's ego? I became a reflection of the hurt and pain that was projected on me. You've heard the phrase "Hurt people, hurt people?" Yeah, I hurt a lot of people, and for no reason. People who never did anything to me. I just found amusement in causing other people torment. That's how low I thought of myself. It's really sad when you think about it. I was screaming on the inside for my hurt to be acknowledged, validated, and to disappear, and since I never received those things, I just went around being mean to people instead. I'm not proud of that in any way but what I want you to understand here is that there is always a reason as to why people do the things they do. I lacked compassion for myself because some people close to me lacked compassion for me. Is it a wonder why I had none for anyone else? It was a horrible cycle that I didn't see needed to be broken. How can I truly extend love to you if I can't extend it to myself?

Because I didn't have the capacity to love myself, I not only disrespected others, but I disrespected myself as well. I allowed people to treat me horribly, all because I didn't think I was worthy of real love and respect. Maybe I just couldn't tell the difference because I didn't know what to look for. I desperately craved love and found myself in some really awful relationships and situations because of it. There is an "a-ha" moment in here. The very people who teased me and left scars on me were probably hurting too, in their own way from their own trauma. So many people walk around with wounds and inflict all kinds of hurt on others. The one thing we can't do is be responsible for someone else's pain. We also are not responsible for their healing. What we are responsible for is our own self-perception DESPITE how others treat us. We must always love ourselves FIRST with the same lens that God loves us through.

Let me say this again: I am in no way an expert on pain, healing, counseling, or anything else you may get from this book. I am not a Pastor, nor am I here to preach the word of God. I am simply a woman who's been through some things that at one point in my life, I thought I'd never heal from. Through God's grace, time, and reflection, I am able to look back at these moments and analyze them differently now. I can see exactly where God was speaking to me, where he intentionally sent healing or direction, and I can see the purpose for my pain.

It was to get me right here, to be a help to some other young woman out there who may feel like they are the ONLY one on the planet feeling this way. That's how I felt. I felt alone like no one could possibly understand. Hell, most days, I didn't even understand what I felt or why. It doesn't feel good when you are going through it, I know… but it feels so good to look back on your growth once you have climbed to the other side of that hill.

My internal struggles followed me through high school and into college. What I want you to understand here is that people are dealing with things that they aren't talking about. What someone thinks of you is NOT your business. You can't make someone see your value and your worth if they don't, but also don't give them the power to change your own perception of yourself. Don't waste years of your life feeling like you aren't good enough, like you aren't pretty enough, like you aren't smart enough, to be treated with respect. Stand up and make them respect you, then walk away knowing that it doesn't matter what they think anyway. The only opinion that truly matters is God. He gave you life and will make that life beautiful and full of happiness if you allow him to. That's what he wants for you. You have to know that you are beautiful. You are worthy of love. You are brilliant and were meant to do something so amazing with this beautiful life God gave you. Life doesn't always feel good. There will be moments where you will feel powerless, but you will not be defeated as long as you keep moving forward.

"And Because God is the greatest power, we shall never be defeated"

-Rich Tolbert Jr.

Every decision we make in life has consequences, good or bad. In every single choice I made where I didn't consult with God first, it ended with pain and/or confusion. God is not the author of confusion, and that in itself should help you understand if you are being led by the spirit or being led by the flesh. Thank God for grace and new mercies every day that he gives us because I was a total train wreck some days. Most young adults are simply trying to figure it out. Hell, most adults are just trying to figure it out. Life is ever-changing. You go through new seasons, so you're ALWAYS trying to figure something out. Sometimes it's a bumpy road, and that's ok. As long as you get it, no matter how long it takes. I have spent many days questioning whether I had strayed too far away from God for him to even think of me, let alone love me. But even during the times, I wasn't close to God, in my heart, I knew he was still there. I knew he was still covering me but I was ashamed to talk to him. I felt so dirty, and I felt like I had dishonored him too badly. That is the farthest thing from the truth. If you feel like that, like you have done too much wrong to turn back to God, know that you could NEVER do too much where God is not waiting to scoop you up in his arms and love on you. Jesus paid the ultimate price for all our sins; he sacrificed his life. There's nothing you can do to separate yourself from the love of God. You just have to choose him. That's it. Choose God.

I am thankful for EVERY moment I have endured and overcome. I have grown so deep in love with God I sometimes feel like I'm looking down on myself, watching myself. Whenever I am challenged or storms come my way, I know without question I have God fighting for me. Declaring a victory over obstacles that you at the time think you'll never make it out of should stir something in your spirit telling you that God is with you in everything you do. At least it does for me when I look back on certain moments. Even the act of God providing peace when the noise around me is so stifling. That's his love on display. Our minds are the devil's playground when our hearts are not postured on God. For me to know there were years where God was not my first, second, or third thought in my day, and everything around me was visibly going wrong, and he still shielded me from dangers seen and unseen while bringing me peace enough to continue on with life is enough for me to praise him as soon as I open my eyes every morning. On my BEST day, I'll still be filthy… and God will love me just the same as he did on my worst day. And for that alone, I will forever worship. You know, worship brings so much peace and clarity to your mind. I stay postured in worship. All day. ALL DAY. Try it and watch your life change.

Chapter 3

My Heart To Yours

Dear young black man,

I know your road is tough

The world wants you to hate yourself

And tells you, you're not enough.

But they're wrong, you're a fighter!

Keep your eyes to the sky.

And when the world goes low,

YOUNG KING, you keep your head held high!

You're the son of a mighty God,

An UNDEFEATED champion.

And he's got a plan for that life of yours...

God's will be done.

Be wise enough to recognize

When the enemy tries to attack.

Let worship be your weapon

And son, God will fight back.

Most of all, I LOVE YOU!

And though the world can be unkind..

The son of God died for all of us,

I'd gladly lay down my life for mine.

Chapter 4

Keshawn Dionté

After I graduated High School, I was extremely excited to go off to college, simply to put some space between me, everything and everyone I knew. Being the baby and the only girl has its perks, but not many. Mostly it was a lot of over sheltering and not being allowed to do basic things any high school student would want to do. I snuck and did a lot of things and was okay with facing the consequences. At the moment, I just wanted to be a normal kid. I went to one of the best high schools in the city; I had great friends … it's not like we were out stealing cars or breaking into stores. Literally, it would be simple stuff like going to the movies or a party. When I got to college, I was looking forward to the freedom than anything else in the world. How did I handle it, you ask? Well, I didn't. I didn't handle it well at all actually. LOL. Since I could now make my own decisions with no one there to tell me no, I made all the wrong ones. I did all the stuff I wasn't allowed to do back home in Chicago, in excess… I hurt some really great people along the way with some of those decisions. You see, giving someone headstrong free reign to do whatever they wanted after not being allowed to do anything for their entire lives was a recipe for disaster. I was selfish in most of my behavior, not thinking about God, the people in my life that cared about me, or what was going to happen next. I was enjoying not being told what I could or could not do, and beyond that, there was no thought process. There was one person in particular whom my decisions hurt the most. The pain I caused will stay with me forever. Even though we eventually moved past everything, I realize the shame of some of my decisions was still eating away in my heart, and I allowed them to take advantage of that. Forgiveness isn't always the other person forgiving you… it's you forgiving yourself and understanding you're not that same person. Seasons have changed. Growth has taken place, and regardless of any pain you've caused, that's not a burden you have to keep carrying around. Give it to God. For me, it has always been so much easier to forgive others than it has been to forgive myself. Do you ever feel like that? I think for me, it's because it means stripping away all the excuses you've convinced yourself validated your decisions. Not to mention that some decisions not only affect a moment, it affects a lifetime. So, when you have that weight bringing you down, it's easier to just patch up the situation instead of healing the situation within yourself.

When I got to Jackson State University, I can't say that my focus was 100% where it should have been. My mind was all over the place. I could finally breathe, but maybe a little too much. I met my son's father in that first year, and things moved rather quickly with us. It seems like I blinked my eyes a few times and I was pregnant; the result of being a little too care free with no structure. This wasn't something I planned, but my behavior also wasn't doing anything to avoid it either. I never considered that the choices I was making in the moment would affect my forever. As I said, I was living from moment to moment.

So now I was about to become a mom. I've always wanted to be a mom, not this young though. Ever since I can remember, I wanted to have children of my own. I dreamed of how I would raise my kids, how I would provide for them... I imagined my husband and I would be the most amazing parents. We'd be so in love and love our kids with the full immensity of our hearts. And they would have the happiest of childhoods. Our home would be full of laughter and beautiful memories. After all, I'd learned from my own parents what to do and what NOT to do, right? I think on some level, this is the fairytale all little girls (who dream of a family) dream of. What I didn't expect was to begin this journey at the age of 18. Yeah, I was terrified! ABSOLUTELY!! This was not the plan. I was still a kid myself; how could I be having one? How did I let this happen? And how was I ever going to make it out alive? My parents are going to kill me! These were the nonstop thoughts in my head at the time.

I had just left college a few months before. The life I thought I wanted turned out not to be the life I was living, and I made the decision to go back. To my surprise, that's when I found out I was pregnant. Ladies, isn't that how it happens? As soon as you make the decision to change your life, end that relationship, step up and make better decisions, you find out you're pregnant. I was so scared to tell my parents. Afraid of what they were going to think of me. They were already so upset that I left college, and rightfully so. At 18, the first time out on your own, you think you have life all figured out. What a lie that is! At 18, YOU KNOW

NOTHING! I KNEW NOTHING! And now, in my mind, I had just completely ruined my life.

My pregnancy wasn't the easiest. The stress of it all caused some health issues that put me on bed rest for almost all of it. And of course, my parents were less than happy. My mom could not even utter the words pregnant for most of my pregnancy. I lost their love and support for good. I was sure of it. On top of the stress I already was under, I was told early on that my child had a strong possibility of having down syndrome. I literally was devastated at the thought of this. Could I handle that? It was already going to be an extreme challenge having a child this young. I already didn't know I was going to maneuver the rest of my life. I needed to know for sure. I took a series of tests, each one riskier than the last to either confirm or deny a positive result. The most accurate test was going to be the amniocentesis, but it also was the most dangerous. My doctor warned that there was a possibility that if I took the test, it would send me into early labor. Still, I needed to be sure, so I took the test.

Now, this was a very reflective time for me. This pregnancy was not planned, but still, it was God's gift. And now there I was waiting to hear whether my son was going to have a genetic disorder that would affect him for the rest of his life. I prayed to God to allow my baby boy to be healthy. I asked God if there was anything I had done to cause this, please don't let my son suffer the consequence. I begged and begged God to allow my baby to be born without this disorder. And all I could do now was wait. Waiting. The time between taking tests and waiting for results is the most mind wrecking moment. You think the worst. It's hard to see your way out of the darkness. For me, anyway. I didn't know God then like I know him now. There was nothing anchoring me to ground while everything was falling apart. God was there, no doubt, but I didn't know it. I couldn't see him because I didn't know what to look for.

After a week and a half, the doctor called with the results of the amnio. Negative!! The results were NEGATIVE!! My son was perfect. I was so happy. God had heard me. My son would not suffer. This was the first moment I felt maybe things would be ok after all. Maybe I wasn't alone in this. I began to get things in order for him.

Around 7 months, I went for a regular checkup. I had a bit of a headache that morning but didn't think anything of it. Headaches were normal. I had an Asian doctor. Totally irrelevant to the story. But he was very kind to me during my pregnancy. I'm sure he could tell how scared I was. My son's father lived in Orlando and as I stated my parents weren't happy about the pregnancy so I never asked them to come to my appointments. I really went through everything alone, looking back on it, and coming to my appointments alone, I think my doctor made sure to show a little more empathy towards me. I don't remember his name, but Thank You sir! Your kindness to me will never be forgotten.

I remember him that day asking all his routine questions. One in particular: have you noticed any discharge. I said no, not giving it a second thought. A few minutes later, it hit me that I did notice a discharge the day before, but these are normal for women, so there was no cause for concern. Still, I had the "urge" to tell him. He said, "Ok, I'm sure it's nothing, but let's test it." As he checked the discharge to see if it was from the baby, he also took my blood pressure again. He left the room for a few minutes and when he came back, he checked my blood pressure again. Then he left. By now, I am freaking out! What was going on? The next person to come in was one of the nurses. She took my blood pressure again, and the look on her face made me numb. The doctor came back in and he sat me up. He told me that the discharge was from the fluid around my baby. It was leaking and my blood pressure was rising at an alarming rate, thus the reason for taking it so many times. He said I would need to get to the hospital to deliver immediately because if we wait, "you and your baby could die."

My entire throat sunk into my ankles. I started crying and shaking. I was so scared. My doctor talked me through what was happening. Again, he was very delicate in how he handled me. He told me go home and pack a bag and have someone drive me to the hospital. I literally lived two blocks from the hospital. I drove home and my mom was there. I told her what happened and that I had to get to the hospital. "He said me and the baby are gonna die!" I said to her hysterically. My mom told me to go pack my bag and let's head up there. Now mind you, I'm only 7 months at this point. So, in addition to the current issue going on, it's too early to deliver a healthy baby! Or so I thought. I got checked in about 7pm, got to my room, and waited in complete fear of what was happening. They came in at some point and gave me the epidural. My nurse was the best. She was so warm and tender with me. I truly believe God sends you angels to help you in your toughest times. She was definitely one of them. My mom said she'd be back in the morning, so now it was just me, the beeping of the machines, and the stillness of the night sky I could see outside of my window. I don't think I slept at all. I cried most of the night. Maybe it was the fear of losing the baby along with my own life, maybe it was because at that moment I should have been enjoying my sophomore year at #THEE Jackson State University with the love of my life, or maybe it was because I was alone in that cold, dark-room, and in that solitude, it made me realize how alone I have ALWAYS felt trying to maneuvering through the difficult moments in life.

The morning was hectic. Doctors, nurses, checking the machines... it was a rat race. My mom came back and sat in a chair out of the way but in my view. Having her there made it feel like everything was going to be alright. The actual delivery process took a total of maybe 30 minutes. I felt nothing until my baby boy's head started crowning. I begin to panic from all the voices, the monitors beeping, the pain, the thought that we might not make it. “Mommy, can you come hold my hand?” I said to my mother, feeling as small as I was when I needed her to hold my hand walking into preschool for the first time at McCann Day Care. “You’re ok, you’ve got your nurses,” she said. I was crushed. That alone feeling I had felt all night instantly came over me. I fought back the tears as best as I could. The sweet nurse from the day before came into the room. She grabbed my hand, smiled at me, and said, “Ok, are you ready to push?” I looked up at her, eyes watering, heart racing. “I’m scared,” I said to her.

“It’s ok. Squeeze my hand as hard as you can and push down.”

Two pushes and my little 5lb 3oz nugget was born. He was so beautiful!! Head full of jet-black hair (explains the heartburn), blue eyes (yes, he’s black), and was just the sweetest little thing I had ever seen. Had it not been for the fact that they cleaned him up and put our matching bracelets on us all in my room, I would have been CERTAIN they switched him with another child! LOL! I had never seen anything more precious in my entire life. I would watch him sleep, just to make sure he was real. How could God trust me with something so perfect? I was a total mess. I would for sure screw this (motherhood) up too! I wasn’t capable of being a mother! Afterall, I was still a child myself. I had no idea what I was doing, and I was terrified.

So quick recap. My parents weren't happy I had just had a baby. My relationship with his father wasn't exactly pleasant. I wasn't in school. My life was completely upside down. I never got the chance to breastfeed my son because he wouldn't latch on. That made me super sad. I wanted that bonding experience that I always heard and read was so important. Not only did I want it, I needed it. I needed something to hold on to, something to give me hope that everything would be ok. Regardless of the circumstances, I was determined to be the best mother I could be, without reservation, and now in my mind, my own baby doesn't like me. Post-partum kicked in pretty hard for me at that point. I didn't feel connected to anything. Not even to myself. I was just going through the motions. I felt so empty… every day… all day. Nothing made that feeling go away. I felt as if I was in the middle of a lake drowning, and although I knew I was going under, I couldn't find the will to do anything but allow the water to submerge me. I felt lost; I felt alone. Like it had been my whole life, I felt I had to keep this to myself.

Listen! I want to break the thoughts in your mind that tell you there's no one out there to reach out to for help. Sometimes we find ourselves in a position where we aren't close to family. Maybe we think our friends will judge us or just couldn't understand because they aren't experiencing the same thing. All that could be facts. It was for me. But there is always someone out there. There's nothing wrong with talking with a counselor or life coach to help you process your thoughts. Some people are skeptical of therapist, but all they do is allow you a safe space to walk through your own thoughts. Sometimes it takes talking to someone who doesn't know you, doesn't have any attachment to you, and doesn't have a stance on what you may be going through in order for you to open up and just allow your thoughts to flow.

For the next few months, I felt like I was outside of my body, watching me live my life and care for my baby. Then one day, my son got hurt and my whole world shifted. We were living in Orlando at the time. He was 3 months old and he broke his leg. Seeing my sweet baby boy in a world of pain that I couldn't take away was heartbreaking. He was in a cast for 6 months. From that moment on, he was glued to my side. I didn't want anyone to hold him. It would forever be me and my sweetness. And my love for him overtook my heart in a way like never before. My mommy instincts were finally kicking in and the post-partum was fading. So, to all the moms out there who don't quite feel like themselves after having their baby, know that you are not alone. About 50% of women go through at least a mild case of it. Our bodies go through physical and hormonal changes. Don't put too much pressure on yourself to feel like the old you. After all, you have shed that life and stepped into a new one: Motherhood! Embrace that!

My son had a very stable life growing up. His dad and I divorced when he was 3; however, he has always been an amazing father to him. Did we go through our fair share of issues, of course, we did. But the one thing I NEVER did was try and hinder their relationship. I would like to be able to say I took the high road and didn't want to be that kind of woman who keeps the child from their father, but the reality is that it never even crossed my mind. That's just not who I am. Literally never once thought about that. Like I said, he's always been a great dad, loves my son to death. Why would I jump in the way of that? My son needs a man to teach him man things. Simple!

All and all, it was a journey having a child so young. I didn't plan it, and I was not prepared for it. But to be honest, he saved my life. He gave me purpose. Everything was for him. All my love belonged to him. I've never been prouder of anything I've done in my entire life! I did that! I created someone as sensitive and loving as me, and his kindness is inspiring. He is so intelligent and talented. I'm in awe everyday of how beautiful his heart and soul really are. More importantly, the one thing that I had done that I thought destroyed my life, saved my life. And the world did not end just because I had a child at a young age. Were there some hard years, yes of course! And I ABSOLUTELY believe that young adults should have things in order, including a plan, finances and maturity, before having a child. But just because something is hard doesn't mean you will fail at it. Even on the darkest of days, you HAVE to remember that the sun will shine again. You have to keep going through. Don't stop, and don't look back. Just keep moving forward and all your storms will pass. God will not fail you. But you've got to do your part. You have to believe in him. Remember: "Because God is the greatest power, we shall never be defeated." -Rich Tolbert Jr. (Just keep reading, I will eventually explain why Rich and this masterpiece of an album is so special.)

My son and I lived in the same house in the same subdivision ever since he was in preschool. Going to school and working full time was a lot! My parents had my son more than I did for a couple of years. By the time I picked him up, he was fast asleep and I may not have gotten any time with him that whole day, but he was in the best care. In fact, I sometimes question if my mom didn't birth my baby! LOL, They LOVE that little man so much. And he completely adores his mama and pawpaw. My parents were the most amazing help to us. We could not have done it without them.

Pause...

Did you catch that? I'll say it again. My parents were the most amazing help to us! The same parents I had disappointed over and over and OVER again. The same parents I thought couldn't possibly love me the same way! The same parents whose love I thought I had surely lost made sure my son and I were never in a position to want for anything. Regardless of how many mistakes I had made, I was forever their child, and they were still going to be there, disappointments and all! Kind of like how we are always disappointing God, but he never stops showing up for us. He keeps on providing, even when we don't know why. He keeps on protecting, no matter how many foolish decisions we make. He keeps on loving us, no matter how many times we turn our backs on his love. He waits patiently, each and every time for us to come back to him, and he loves us just the same. See, you have to remember that God made the ULTIMATE sacrifice for us. He sacrificed his only son, Jesus, JUST for us. He knows we are imperfect people; sinners, all of us, and still he sent his son Jesus to pay the cost for those sins, not even knowing if we would accept God into our lives! WHOA! Let me say that again! God sent his son to die for us on a MAYBE we would choose him! And many people still don't. But he still loves us all and is ready to take us into his arms if/when we DO choose him. I get emotional thinking about that. How could you not love a God that loves you that much? He deserves more of us… he deserves ALL of us.

Chapter 5

The Pursuit of Happiness.

There was a period of my life where I was undeniably reckless, and I am so thankful to God for his protection during that time. When you're young, you don't consider how your actions have consequences. You don't think of all the people affected by your decisions. You're often selfish in your behavior, only thinking of momentary joy. Even though I had a child, and his needs came far above everything else, I still was selfish in my decisions that could potentially affect his life. It was never my intention to be this way, but maturity comes with age. One night in particular will stay with me forever. This is the night God showed himself in full Glory.

I lived outside the city, about 25 minutes from everything. Not far, but not exactly around the corner. I was on my way home from a night out with friends. I had way more drinks than I should have, but that wasn't uncommon. The way my body's set up, I'm fine up until the 3 or 4 minutes before my exit ramp. Then sleepy time comes over my body and I start drifting into slumber. This night was no different. It was about 3 in the morning. No one on the highway but me. I felt myself getting sleepy, but I told myself I was ok. I was NOT ok, because I must have blinked a little too hard and dozed off. My car veered off to the right, slightly on the shoulder. As my tires hit the shoulder, it woke me up suddenly in a panic and I swerved the wheel to the left. At this point, my car is in a 360 spin on the interstate. I spin once… I spin twice… and I'm approaching the concrete wall that divides the highway. In my mind, I know I am going to die. There's nothing to save me. I instantly thought of my son. Now everything seems to move in slow motion. I clinched the steering wheel as hard as I could. I said aloud, "God, I love you… Keshawn, I love you," as I am now almost face to face with the wall. I closed my eyes, still gripping the wheel…. And nothing. A few seconds later, I open my eyes, and my car is in park on the right shoulder. I looked around. I began grabbing my arms, my face, my legs in an effort to reaffirm to myself I was still alive. I sat there for a moment, and I put my car in drive and proceeded on my travel home.

I was ALIVE! God supernaturally reached down his hand and saved my life. At this point in my life, I was not close to God, so I would have loved to given credit to a more explainable reason for why I was not dead, but there simply wasn't one. God did that. He saw fit to save me. I was WORTH saving! He loved me enough to save me! ME! And guess what? I didn't even thank him. He saved my life, and I didn't even say 'Thank you God' before I put my car in drive and drove off. That has plagued me for some years now. How selfish I was. I undoubtedly knew I was only saved by God, but at the moment, I only thought of myself. Still selfish, although I knew better. Over the next few months, there was a tugging at my spirit. There were about 3 other moments where I can tell you God intervened with his protection. And it was in THOSE moments that I was reminded of how much he loved me. Those moments approaching the wall kept flashing in my mind. Even now, I can see and feel it as if

I'm still in the car and my heart begins to race. When you stare death in the eye and able to come out on the other side, it changes you. I didn't get it right away, but it didn't take long. God has me here for an assignment so specific that he could NOT let me die! There is purpose for my life! There is a reason why God saved me. So now, let me tell you about my friend Rich.

In 2020, Rich Tolbert Jr. released the most profound and life-changing song called "I'm Alive" on his album entitled "Never Be Defeated." Quick background, after a lifetime of questioning his own existence, one night, he stared death in the eye himself, making the decision to take his own life. He was very thorough in his decision, even taking time out to write personal notes to certain people in his life so there would be no question as to why he did this and detailing how he wanted his funeral to be. Rich describes feeling the life leaving his body and everything going dark. The next morning, he opened his eyes and realized he was still here. The first words out of his mouth were, "I'm alive!" Our heavenly father allowed him to rise the next morning with new grace and a song in his heart. He instantly wrote the entire song, still dazed from the night before. God physically would not allow him to die! The assignment designed for his life was so specific that he could NOT die before fulfilling it. You see, we are all here not for ourselves but to help someone else on their journey. I truly believe that! I read something once that said, "remember to extend grace because we're all just walking each other home." That statement in my opinion, is the sum of what we all should aspire to do.

God Knows the plans he has for me...
He knows the thoughts he thinks towards me.
And nothing is an accident...
I'm ALIVE BECAUSE THERE'S MORE!!
He didn't let me die, let me die...
He didn't let me die, let me die...
And THIS is not an accident.
I'M ALIVE BECAUSE THERE'S MORE!!
-Rich Tolbert Jr.

Doesn't that just give you chills? I mean, just think about it for a second. You have it made up in your mind that there is nothing more in this life worth pressing on for. You're sure of this. You have crossed all your T's... and dotted all your I's, as my mama would say. You create this cocktail of death and wait for death to come get you. And what happens? Jesus shows up and says, "Nah, this is not going to happen today. I got other things planned for you, and maybe now that I've saved your life, you'll understand that." Whew! I don't know how else I can make it clear that when God has an assignment for you, it is one that he will see you through until the end. And let's be clear, we all have an assignment. What humbles me is that Rich is so open and honest about the experiences he has gone through. How many men or women of God do you hear boldly telling you about their battles with depression, attempts of suicide, or history of molestation? Some, yes. But not many. I think that's why this album Never Be Defeated is so powerful. It allows you a space to confront the pain you may have kept hidden inside of yourself. Again, so many people are walking around with mountains and mountains of weight sitting right on their hearts and wonder why it's a struggle to function day to day. Rich penned an album that declares victory over defeat in all things simply because God is the greatest power. "I'm Alive Because There's More." That statement gives language to a wave of emotions that I have carried for over 10 years. If you know me personally, then there's a chance you have heard this story before. And each time I have told it, I always say I don't know why God saved me, but I'm glad he did. Now I have words to convey how I feel. Now I know why God saved me. It's simple: BECAUSE THERE'S MORE!

God would not let me die because there was more in store for me! There was more for me to do. More for me to accomplish. More for me to learn. More for me to experience. THERE'S MORE! There's a reason I'm still here. THERE'S MORE! This song has given me an answer for the rest of my life, and I am forever changed by it. "Nothing is an accident. I'm alive because there's more." For all I've been through, THERE'S STILL MORE! For all the hurt, THERE'S STILL MORE! All the betrayal, THERE'S MORE! The disappointments, THERE'S STILL MORE! I want to encourage you the way Rich has encouraged me every single day since I first heard I'm Alive.

Keep going, know that God's plans are good. They are not meant to harm you. And he will allow it all to work in your favor. He never said bad things wouldn't happen. He never promised you would be healthy, financially secure or successful. But what God promises is to never leave you and that you'd have his grace… and that grace would be enough to get you through anything you encounter. I am so thankful for Rich, and I'm glad God wouldn't let him die. What God has done and is going to continue to do in his life is going to be so amazing! I believe that. There's more! God had more for him. God had more for me. And God has more for you too. Believe in him.

After this experience, I began to take life a little more seriously. I began to think about the future, what I wanted to do, who Keke was created to be. I always made sure my son lived a very comfortable life. I was working while he was in school, but there was a constant nagging in my spirit that there was more out there for me that I should be doing. I began to consider going back to college, but that would mean going back to almost never seeing my baby, and that's partly why I quit in the first place. Then there was the mere fact that I simply did NOT want to go back. But on the other side of that, not graduating from college was something I couldn't imagine being my reality. I had a lot to think about, and the tugging on my spirit grew stronger and stronger. I come from a very collegiate family. Almost everyone in my family went to Jackson State University, except for my mom who went to Mississippi Valley State, and my dad went to the army. Both my older brothers got their degrees from JSU, and I had completed two years already. It made sense to go back, right? I didn't have a lot going on for real. No real future life plans, so understandably, college was tugging at me.

I remember talking my thoughts over with a dear friend of mine, the very one I had caused so much pain in the beginning of my college career, and he was very adamant about me going back and getting my degree. His opinion meant a lot to me, so of course, I put a lot of thought into it after that. One day, he asked me if I had ever seen "The Pursuit of Happiness", a movie starring Will Smith. I hadn't seen it yet, but he gave it great reviews. He is a harsh critic, so if he says something is good, it must be spectacular. Lol. A few months later, I was sitting at home in the afternoon, watching tv, and I saw it was coming on. At first, I was going to skip over it, but something told me to sit right there and watch it. I can't explain it, but it was an intense feeling. I obediently sat in the corner of my couch and watched. The film touched me in so many different ways. I felt a wave of motivation come over me. It was at that moment I felt I had been doing my life an injustice by simply just surviving. There was so much more out there for me. All I had to do was be focused enough to go after what I deserved. Literally, that film changed my life! The next week, I re-enrolled in Jackson State and got back on track for my degree.

That nagging feeling was God telling me there were things

I needed to accomplish that only having that degree would help facilitate. There were people assigned to my future that I would meet in that collegiate setting. There were learning and growth moments I would need to help me on my journey that I would only get at JSU. Now, don't mistake me. College is not for everyone. There are people doing exceptional in life who have never stepped foot on a college campus. And that's awesome! I am only walking you through MY journey. FOR ME, this was a necessary step for my life plan that God set out for me. I think there is something so beautiful about a collegiate setting. It's not all about the classes you're required to take because let's be honest, Biology and Calculus will never come up in my day-to-day life. But the life and social skills you pick up being around so many culturally diverse individuals can't be compared. And I'm a strong advocate for my Black young sisters and brothers strongly considering a HBCU. Yes, I wanted my own son to attend a HBCU, preferably JSU like both of his parents, but he chose differently, and that's ok too. The rich history of HBCUs cannot be compared and is often not taught. Not just on a collegiate level, but the true history of the greatness and resilience of Black people is often a footnote, if that, in the history books. If there is one thing I suggest people do their OWN research on is their history. No matter who you are, don't trust solely what you read in one book or what they teach you in school. As I always say, do not let them narrate your story.

Now that I had re-enrolled in school, I was ready to take

my future seriously. I shifted my major slightly to accommodate certain courses I wanted to focus on and I was in a good place. Remember when I told you there were certain people I would meet that were assigned to my future? One person in particular is one of my best friends, Dr. Shawanna Coleman. This life journey we have been on has been since college has been amazing. She has been a shoulder to cry on during all of my dark days (and there have been many), and she has been there to celebrate through all my wins! She doesn't judge but also doesn't give fluff advice. She's going to give it to you straight, no chaser. She has been a true anchor in my life, and I'm so thankful for her sisterhood. We bounce business ideas off of each other and support each other in whatever is in front of us. She is my prayer partner, and at the same time, the one who will pull up and check anyone for stepping wrong! I Love you Shae Cole! Life wouldn't be the same without you!

I graduated from Jackson State University in May of 2010 with a Bachelor's of Science, majoring in Mass Communications with an emphasis in Public Relations and a minor in Graphic Design. After college, I immediately got a job in Advertising. I worked in this industry for 4 years. I didn't particularly enjoy my job, mainly because at the time, I had a supervisor who made my life pure HELL! I have no idea why this man disliked me so much. He was so disrespectful to my face but would tell other people in the office I was wonderful. I can remember a time I went to my HR manager to discuss with her my issues and she said, "That's strange because he tells me you're one of the best people on his team!" That made me so furious; I felt like he was trying to make me look stupid or something! Just manipulative. This was my first touch of the business world though, and it taught me such a huge lesson. People may not like you for absolutely NO valid reason other than they just don't like you. But as long as you do what's required of you to the best of your ability, you'll win. My goal was to put a solid 3 years of corporate work experience on my resume. I did 4. And with the exception of that one particular manager, I picked up a few amazing references. It was never my goal to be there long term. I did what I came to do, and when it was time for me to go, God removed me into the next necessary phase of my life.

I connected with a pretty cool group of young entrepreneurs soon after. Network Marketing was becoming quickly popular and I thought, why not! I stayed really close to my mentor, Solomon Lacy, who is truly one of the most influential people in my life. He taught me what it was to really mentor someone. He pushed and motivated me in not only business but in life in general. The compassion he showed me could not be compared. And he allowed me to trust someone again. Soon, I was mentoring my own group of entrepreneurs, just the way he had mentored me. We had a lot of fun growing through various companies, and we made lots of money along the way. But the connections are what I value the most. Remember, it's not WHAT you know, it's WHO you know. I have had business partners all over, and many of those strong bonds I built then, I still value today. What I learned about the power of Networking and being fearless when talking with people is what has driven every moment of my life since then.

I could go on and detail every step of my professional career, but the details aren't important. I've had a lot of success in almost everything I have put my hands on. I've gotten the attention of VPs and CEOs of my companies without that being my goal. The thing that has allowed me to slingshot to the forefront of my peers, I believe, is my personality and willingness to give 110% with a smile. I'm a strong advocate for respect. No one has the right to be disrespectful to another person, no matter what the situation. Respect is earned, not given. One thing I always say is you don't have to like me; you don't even have to respect me, but what you won't do is disrespect me. I simply don't feel it is necessary to behave badly. It doesn't make you look better to be condescending or try and flex your authority. I take pride in the fact that I handle people with care and compassion. Mostly because, as I told you, I haven't always been this way. God had to renew me to use me. He stripped me down and built me back up. I often think back on how cruel I was to people and how broken I was on the inside that caused me to behave that way. This is also why I handle people with care. You never know what someone else is dealing with, what kind of hurt or trauma they are carrying around.

Here's the important thing to remember. God will put the people in your life that have the ability to help you along your journey, people who are in a position to move you to the front simply because God's grace wants you there. You have to still do your part though. You have to treat people right. You have to do the work to back up your words. And you have to have the confidence to go out there and get what you deserve. The life you dream of isn't going to just fall in your lap. What God has for you is and will always be for you. But you have to have your eyes and heart open to see it and listen to God's voice. The things I have been able to accomplish in short periods of time I did with ease. Most times, it didn't feel complicated at all. Stop being afraid of actually getting everything you want! Believe in the concept that you can have everything your heart desires. With God, all that you envision is in reach. Afterall, God is the source of all visions.

Chapter 6

Life Is Worth the Fight

My mom has been telling me for as long as I can remember that I love EVERYONE more than I love myself. I give, and give, and give to other people, not thinking of the damage I may be doing to myself or even caring about my own feelings. For a long time, I had no clue of what she meant. I just love how I love. Was that a bad thing? Was I supposed to be something I wasn't? To me, the way I care for people is normal. Aren't all people like this? Don't all people just naturally love this hard? Questions that I'd ask myself every time she said that to me before I understood WHY she was saying it to me. This is when I found out.

Dating is such a beautiful thing. Most times, it's fun and exciting! That butterflies in your stomach feeling... the random thoughts in the middle of the day that makes you smile from ear to ear for a solid 3 and a half minutes... checking your phone every 15 minutes to make sure you didn't miss a text from your boo. Date night. Baecations. (That's a vacation with your significant other for those of you that don't live in social media world). Having someone you're really into is one of the sweetest, purest feelings that can exist. I remember that feeling fondly. And it's a feeling I had always chased after.

I was in a particular relationship for 4 years. We seemed to have all the same things in common in the beginning. We both loved music and art... We'd have the longest conversations about nothing and everything. He seemed to just 'get me' in a way no one had before. You know that feeling. When you're just smiling all day, crazy in love, don't want to be without them for even 5 minutes. That type of love. The first year and a half were great, or so that is what I thought then. Maybe it's because somewhere along the way, we become blind and a little too forgiving to what's in front of us. He started changing; little by little, more and more. He became unfamiliar to me. He no longer was this great guy I longed to be near in the beginning of our relationship. I began to make excuses for his behavior: "he's just stressed about work." I blew off his behavior, trying to be supportive and not add additional drama. How many of you have ever dismissed what you felt because you just didn't want to deal with the drama or argue? Let's normalize NOT doing that! Those feelings are your intuition telling you something is off. "Intuition" is simply another way of saying Holy Spirit. The Holy Spirit is trying to tell you something. We should listen to these little nudges. It's God's way of guiding us. Often, we disregard it and end up regretting it.

Those moments were probably the biggest mistakes I could have made for what was to come. Looking back now, there were signs all around me. I just wasn't open to the warnings that maybe, JUST maybe, this was NOT the right guy for me. If you learn nothing else from reading about my lessons through life, please remember to pay attention to the signs and those little nudging feelings that won't leave. Again, God always sends you guardian angels to lead and protect you. He will communicate with you through dreams, through people, what seems to be random conversations, memories, or even visions and premonitions. It's all God expressing his love for you and trying to guide you through life. The question is will you pay attention.

Time went on and my guy got cold. I was no longer receiving the attention from him that I normally had. He began to get paranoid about everything. He thought people were following him. He was convinced I was cheating on him with his friends (some of which I had never even met before). He was irritated ALLLLL the time, which in turn frustrated me. I just didn't understand what was happening. One day in particular, we were in the kitchen arguing. Now, I can't remember what I said, but as I walked away, he began to laugh hysterically. For 2 minutes straight, I sat there and watched this man laugh continuously after we were JUST in WW3! It was the strangest thing I'd ever witnessed. I walked away, feeling a chill overcome my entire body. I somehow KNEW something just shifted and he was no longer himself.

Ok, so you're probably reading this thinking, "Keke did this really happen?" I wish I could tell you that I added a little bit of fiction in here, but this actually happened, and this was only the beginning. We were now approaching year 3. After that day in the kitchen, his behavior got more erratic. Nights were the worst. I'd lay in bed trying to go to sleep. One minute he'd be awake, seemingly just fine. Next minute he'd be silently laughing, looking to both sides as if something were next to him other than a wall. This would go on all night. After the first night, I knew I couldn't be in that room with him. The next night, I went to the couch. I watched TV until I dozed off to sleep, keeping one ear on the laughs coming from under my bedroom door. I'd pop in the room randomly a few times... opening the door quietly and slowly so that I'd see him before he had a chance to see me. The laughing only stopped when I'd walk into the room.

During the day, my guy was himself... at first. Then one day, I came home and he was on the back patio. The house was quiet, so I could hear the mumbles of his voice and then I saw his shadow behind the patio door. I peaked through the blinds to see if he was alone. He was, but what I saw next froze me in my tracks. Picture two people having an intense conversation. You can imagine their body language, facial expressions, hand gestures. All of it right? Now Imagine it only being one person in this conversation. You see all of the body language, facial expressions, hand gestures, and let's not forget the person is actually having a conversation, you just can't see the person they're talking to. Can you imagine all that? Ok, let's continue.

All that you just imagined is what I saw through the blinds. I was speechless! I was terrified! I ran out of the house, got into my car and drove off. Now, don't think for a second that through all this I wasn't asking him what was wrong or what was making him act like this. But often, you can't tell someone with mental health issues that they have a problem. For them, they are normal. There were multiple times I called the police. One of the last times I called the police on him, they kept him in lock up for about 30 days. Before he was released, he agreed to visit a doctor with me to figure out what was going on. I did not want to give up on him, although I was literally in fear every day. For some reason, I felt compelled to "fix" him. Isn't that crazy? Ladies, why do we often feel like it's our job to fix our men? Grown men? Men, you are not exempt. There are many men who are in relationships with women they feel obligated to help. We stay way past our expiration date and then wonder why we are unhappy every day. We feel an obligation to someone that God tells us we have no future with. We must learn God's voice, so we recognize it when he speaks. When he tells you it's time to let that go, you must obey.

At some point, my guy began to be angry all the time. His paranoia grew stronger. And shortly after, the physical abuse began. Now, I know you're probably wondering why I didn't just cut my losses and move on. Well, there are a number of reasons. None of them should have been enough to disregard my own health and safety, but nevertheless, I did. The obvious being that I loved him. And you may ask how could you continue to love someone who treats you so bad... I wish I had an answer for you. But one thing is for sure; abuse starts mentally before it ever gets physical. You see, he would always make me feel like a horrible person for even suggesting that we break up... like I was giving up on him like my love had been a lie all along. Like I didn't deserve love or happiness in the future because what kind of person would leave someone so devoted to them as he was? This is what manipulation looks like.

Mental manipulation is a stronghold you don't even see coming. It can hit you all at once or creep into your psyche over time. And if you aren't strong, you'll succumb to the pull. I wasn't emotionally strong. So, I fell into the fold. He was set off by anything. And let's not forget that there was the presence of his personality splitting. The first time he hit me, I was in rage. I mean, we were blow for blow! There was no time to think about anything. You just react. When things calmed down, I locked myself in my guest room and cried for about 5 hours straight. How the hell is this my life? I just couldn't understand. He knocked on the door for hours, begging to come in. Somewhere in the middle of the night, I let him in. I sat there silently, weeping. My mind wanted to shout, "WHY DID YOU DO THIS TO ME? GET OUT OF MY HOUSE!" But I couldn't force a word out. "I'm so sorry baby," he said. "It will never happen again." I laid there ashamed of myself, but foolishly, I believed his words.

I woke up the next morning with two black eyes and a bruise on my leg the size of a child's basketball. I was in so much physical pain, but it did not compare to the emotional agony I felt. I think I laid in that bed questioning life for the next couple of days. I couldn't eat, couldn't sleep, couldn't tell anyone. I was just alone. And it was just the beginning.

I could lay out the details of a number of stories like this that happened over the next 6 months. The truth is the outcome was always the same; he was still there. About 2 months after the physical abuse began, I was done. I just wanted him gone, and I let him know. I asked him, told him, demanded and begged him to get out. The relationship was over. I didn't want him there... But he refused. And even suggesting it made him angry. I got up the nerve to go to the police station one day. I told the officer of his mental state and how his personality shifted throughout the day and he had become abusive and he refused to leave my house. I didn't know what else to do. The officer genuinely seemed worried. I had seen him around my city for years, so there was a familiarity with him. What he said next was a total shock to me. He said if he lived in the house for more than 6 months, he's considered a resident and I'd have to take him to court to get him removed. HOW IS THIS POSSIBLE! My house, the bills, NONE of this is in his name. This has been my house for years! This was the law, and at this moment, I realized there is no protection for women in abusive situations. We are on our own. THIS is another reason why women stay.

The officer didn't let it end there though. He said he would gather a team of officers to come to my house with an EMT and they could evaluate the situation at my house. If they saw danger, they'd remove him immediately. We were to meet around the corner from my house in an hour. I drove around for about 45 minutes. Something didn't sit right with me. "IF" they deemed him a danger. No, no, that would not work. He seems normal to an average person. I know when he's different because I know him! I went to the meet up spot and I went up to the officer. I asked him what happens if they got there and didn't find anything out of the ordinary? (as if they knew what ordinary was in my house) "We'll have to leave him there," he said.

To summarize this, I would go to the house with a team of officers and paramedics, questioning whether this man is a danger to me or himself. He fools them into thinking everything is just fine, they leave and I'm alone with a pissed off monster. No way! I could not take that chance. "Call it off! I can't do this, you can't guarantee this will protect me and I can't take that risk, he'll kill me." And I sat in tears as everyone left. What was I going to do now?

From that point on, I would just talk to God and beg him to remove this man from my life. I'd ask him to show me what I got to do to get him out of my house. I avoided him most of the day and at night, I'd sleep in the other room. Imagine that! Sleeping in another room in your own home because you no longer felt safe. Moments when he seemed to be most like himself, I'd cautiously and calmly express to him that I wanted him to leave and there was nothing else to gain out of the relationship. Things were peaceful for about 3 weeks, and then out of nowhere, he looked at me and said, "Fine, if you don't want me here, I'll leave!" He packed all his things, and he left.

I couldn't believe it, but finally, I was free… or so I thought. Remember, abuse begins with mental manipulation. I lived in fear, for the next year at least, looking over my shoulder, not sleeping at night, waiting for him to come back and destroy me and everything in my life. I had become the complete opposite of who I was. I was guarded, afraid, untrusting, angry, sad... PTSD in full effect. I thought there is no way I would ever let someone in again. I didn't trust myself; I didn't trust men anymore. I just wanted to stay to myself. And I did, for the next 4 years. I didn't meet anyone new, refused to even entertain the idea of opening up to someone else again. I put all my focus on everything else. Remember when I told you I got into business with an amazing group of entrepreneurs, and I started network marketing? It was here, and it truly saved my life. My mentor, Solomon, became so much more than a business partner. He became my friend, my brother. He counseled me on things he wasn't even aware of. He motivated me. He pushed me. He encouraged me. He believed in me, and in turn, I started to believe in myself again. This powerful group of people changed how I looked at myself. We were successful in the businesses, but we were even more successful in the connections we built. And that to me, is priceless. Having things are great, but having like-minded people in your corner that push you to be phenomenal is better!

Thank you, Solomon, for being my anchor during one of the most difficult transitions of my life. I love you forever!

God knew what and who I needed at the very moment I needed it. And although I went through that horrible experience, I made it. God never took his hands off my life. He protected me every step of the way, and the wisdom I've gained from that is what counts. This has been the hardest chapter. Going back and facing those memories dropped me to my knees in tears a few times, but I can smile in knowing that hopefully, the woman reading this who may be in a similar situation finds hope and gets the courage to leave. But what I want you to take away from this is that in a season of complete loss of control, I HAD to rely on God. Had I gotten myself in this situation, yes. But God never stopped sending me signs of his love and guidance throughout it, and when I realized I could only depend on him to remove me from this, he did so safely. And literally all at once. You see, my fear for my safety kept me there, and because I wasn't strong enough to remove myself from the situation on my own, God changed my ex's mind and made him leave. That's how much my father loved me! I know there are some of you who are reading this and saying, "couldn't be me," "I would've done this" or "I would've done that". Let me assure you that you never know what you would do until you are actually in that situation. I always said it wouldn't be me either. You can judge me, that's ok. I'll accept it. It's all a part of my journey and I'm no longer living in shame of it. But what I do pray is that whoever reads this book shows more empathy and compassion to those in THEIR lives. Someone you know could be living this exact storyline. They could be desperate and aching to tell you what's going on but feel like they can't. It only takes one person to help one person to make this world better. I challenge you to be that one person.

Ladies, we have to know we are worthy of the most tender love that exists. The man God has for you loves you with the intensity that God loves you. He is intentional in his desire to lead you more into the presence of God, not away from God. Find a man that adores you, that wants to help you grow. That encourages you and lifts you up. A man that teaches you is a King. Someone that makes you level up. Someone that makes your house a home. We always hear that the woman makes the house a home, but men you equally share that responsibility. Home is the place you feel safe, the most relaxed, and where you can be your most authentic you. Ladies, a man who gives you this peace is the man you wait for. Settling for anything less is disrespectful to the Queen that you are. It took me 30+ years to learn that. Please learn it early.

Chapter 7

Plain Sight

She was completely covered,
Yes, cloaked by the wind
Hiding from the pain
Consumed with shame from within.
Can't share the pain with no one
Wouldn't dare to tell her friends.
So, she went on every day.
Hiding the pain within.
His rage grew louder and louder...
Her voice got so small.
And to always have been the one to defend the wronged
She seemed to have no voice at all.
Life went on, day by day...
She woke up wondering if it'd be her last
For the man she'd grown to adore
Vowed to permanently prison her in the past.
24 hours of a tormented cycle
At least 3 she'd come to see.
For the man she loved was hiding
Inside a merry go round of misery.
The rage grew stronger and stronger
The days got longer and longer.
And the rare stillness of the nights' cool air
Were the only time allowed for peaceful wonder.
She can still remember his face

And how the lines on them changes with the soul
No two of them resembled each other
Even the rumble of his voice wasn't known.
And it got harder to hide the bruises
Black eyes lingering behind shades.
In her world that should have been black or white
There were all these shades of grey...
And each night, as she laid down her head
As rivers flowed from her eyes
She just wanted it all to be over
As the silence deafened her cries.
She couldn't share the pain with no one
Wouldn't dare to tell her friends.
So, she went on every day.
Hiding the pain within.

Chapter 8

Transformation

2020 was a special kind of year for SO many reasons. Feel free to allow the term "Special" mean whatever it means to you. The obvious reason being Covid-19. Around the end of February, the first cases started to hit the United States and shortly after, the whole county, most of the world actually, was quarantined at home. Most businesses were forced to shut down. Only industries deemed "essential" were allowed to operate. I was working as a restaurant manager, as I had been for years, so of course we were still open, but because we still had to cut the number of people working. I was put on temporary leave as most of the industry. No problem, I thought. I could use the vacation. No one knew what to expect with this virus, but one thing is for sure, no one expected it to last as long as it had. I ended up being off work for a total of four months. I, like everyone else, stock up on food, toiletries, wine and liquor. My plan was to sleep, eat, drink, binge out on movies and shows, then wake up and do it all over. MY PLAN… God had other plans for me.

I am going to bounce around a little bit in this chapter; just try and follow. It will all make sense in the end. I promise not to lose you.

I love Gospel Music. Without question. I am a HUGE fan of The Walls Group and Jonathan McReynolds. I began to feel my pull to their music stronger at the beginning of quarantine. Of course, I didn't really think anything of it as they both were in heavy rotation on my playlist already. Also, my sleep patten was completely off during this time. I literally would be up all night and finally fall asleep around 6 in the morning. (Anyone else still off center from last year?) Then I'd be right back up at about 11. I wasn't keeping track though, after all, I had nowhere to be. I was drawn to Jonathan McReynolds' "Make Room" for almost a week straight. Once again, this isn't unusual for me because I will wear a repeat button OUT! LOL! My cousins are shaking their heads right now, I'm sure because each one of them has a story about me and a favorite song of mine that I drove them crazy with. ☺ But the song was hitting a part of my heart in a different way. I'd cry EVERY time I listened to it or watch the video; in a GOOD way though. I felt something stirring inside me but still, I didn't really pay it that much attention because I didn't know exactly what it was. Then everything got dark really quickly.

All eyes were on the overwhelming amount of Black people being killed. Breonna Taylor, Ahmaud Arbery, George Floyd and countless others were murdered. Police around the country were showing just how little respect they have for black and brown people. Then all of a sudden, black people were popping up in various places, hanging from trees, every one of them ruled a suicide. The county was in an uproar. It seemed to be every other day I'd open my phone to Instagram or Twitter and see a video of a black person being murdered. There were protests happening in every city. Riots, police using insane amounts of force on peaceful protesters… My heart was breaking. I found myself in tears most of the day and there seemed to be no end in sight. I didn't really have the words to convey what I felt. Only tears and sadness, and with the world in quarantine, the only one I could lean on for comfort was God.

Now, understand, I HAD to give you context to what was going on around me as God prepared me for a shift. The things I've just told have nothing to do with me personally other than laying out a timeline for you, but if I failed to explain my mind frame and the need to hear more of God's voice, you may not see the strength of God's hand.

Now, back to "Make Room." Do you know that song? If not, let me share a few of the lyrics:

"I find space for what I treasure. I make time for what I want. I choose my priorities and Jesus you're my number one. So, I will make room for you. I will prepare for two so you don't feel that you can't live here. Please live in me."

-Jonathan McReynolds

Those lyrics echoed in my head over and over. I began to ask God if he was trying to tell me something. Now, remember when I said I bought lots of wine and liquor to get through the quarantine? During this time, while Make Room was etched in my head, the Lord took away my taste for alcohol. I was extremely confused at first by the whole thing actually, as I enjoy cocktails. And it's not as if I had random liquor; I had what I normally enjoy. Every time I made a drink, I'd take a sip and it would taste horrible. I literally would take a few sips and end up pouring it out because it tasted that bad. ☹ I didn't know what to think of it the first few days. After about a week, I stopped trying. I realized God was trying to talk to me, and I had to be fully coherent to hear his voice.

Darrel Walls, the oldest member of The Walls Group, who also happens to be a Pastor, Song Writer, Producer, the absolute master of vocal arrangements, (oh and cannot forget Grammy Award Winning! LOL) is by far my favorite worship leader of ALL TIMES! The way he ministers to you while ushering you in the presence of God, all while singing the most beautiful and complex melodies is really dope! On March 22th, 2020, a week after everything shut down, including in-person Church, Darrel began Acts Church. What is Acts Church? It is a LIVE worship session on his Instagram live (@musiqcity) that he does every Sunday night. Now, I already loved The Walls Group, and Darrel had done a few live worships on IG already. But he began Acts Church after quarantine shut down in-person Church. That first worship was 2 hours of intimate glory! It was so beautiful; just him, and couple of friends. The tears that flowed let me know God was indeed trying to get my attention. Darrel continued Acts Church the next Sunday and has built an amazing worship experience and community of people who simply want to bask in God's goodness. Not only did Darrel cry out in worship on these lives, but he coached us. He taught us. His transparency with his own struggles in life and how he ultimately made the decision to submit to God was so powerful. And since we were ALL home on lockdown, his live ministering did not stop on Sundays. He would randomly go live throughout the day, all throughout the week, sharing the music he's written and produced in the past and giving us sneaks peaks of new music he was working on. We'd have rap sessions where we could just ask him questions and get to know him better, apart from Darrel of TWG or Darrel the Pastor we all loved. And then he'd just go live and share his thoughts, his private moments with God, and how God speaks to him, especially during a time where we all felt saddened by what was happening around us and we all were trying to figure out how to hear from God more. Acts Church and any random live Darrel did become a necessary part of my day. I realized he was feeding a part of my soul that I didn't know was starving for a closer relationship with God. To this day, whenever he goes live, you better know that I will be on it, ready for the Holy Spirit to have his way through Darrel. And make no mistake, God shows up and moves every single time.

Now, In April, Jonathan McReynolds released a Visual Album called "People." Such a beautiful and soul-grabbing body of work. From beginning to end. And the visuals were amazing. It was what was needed for such a time as this; being in the middle of an unforeseen pandemic with no end in sight, people dying, loved ones getting ill, people out of work, toilet paper shortages (LOL, I'm still not over how some of ya'll acted). It was simply a beautiful album. And then suddenly, it made sense WHY "Make Room" was stuck in my head. God was asking me to make room for Him. He was knocking on the door of my heart, waiting for me to let Him in so He could do necessary work in me. I sat and listened to that song and it had a completely different meaning at that moment. Here's how I began to see it:

We were in the middle of a historical moment where one moment to the next just wasn't promised. If there was ever a time to get closer to God, this was it; and he made it possible to do just that. The world is so busy… our days are filled with work, kids, friends, meetings, travel; everything but God! He stopped the whole world so we could pay attention to him. He took all of our activities away so we could give more of ourselves to him. He wanted us to make Him a priority! God made it easy for us to develop a relationship with Him if we wanted. We no longer had any excuses… we now had the time; all we had to do was make room.

My will (you can move that over)
My way (you can move that over)
My ego (you can move that over)
My plans (you can move that over)
My schedule (you can move that over)
My itinerary (you can move that over)
I WILL MAKE ROOM FOR YOU
My habits (you can move that over)
My attitude (you can move that over)
Whatever it is that's not like you
Whatever it is, you can move over
I will make room

-Jonathan McReynolds

From that moment on, despite what was going on in the world, I KNEW without a doubt that God was using this downtime for me to reconnect with Him. Like Darrel always says, "What God allows, he uses." That was exactly true. No, God didn't cause this pandemic. But that would not stop him from using it for his glory in my life. That is also why he took the taste of alcohol away. He needed me to be able to hear his voice when he spoke. I couldn't have any distractions or anything hindering my consciousness. Wow! God loved me that much! He did all this for me! ☺ I know you're probably saying, "but Keke, He didn't do all this for YOU!" That's where you are wrong. He absolutely did this for me. He did it for you too. The question is, did you hear his voice and make room for him? Did you reconnect with him? Did your will overpower your obedience? See, so many times throughout my life, especially in the last 10 years, God has been tugging on me, waiting on me to build the relationship with him that he longed for. But my own will overpowered his will for me. My obedience was not to God but to my own desires. Once I shifted my posture and let God in, God became my desire. And then things got really good! Jonathan McReynolds sang one of his new songs from his "People" album during Transformation Church, led by Pastor Michael Todd, one Sunday. I was excited because I was already falling in love with Pastor Mike's teaching. That service had me in complete shambles. I'm talking on my knees, begging God to change my life. I knew he had me exactly where he wanted me, surrounded by the people who could reach my heart in the way he needed. God assigns you to certain people in every season of your life that will guide you in your walk with him. If you remember, I told you early on that music has always been a HUGE part of my life. I've always loved Gospel music, but I've always been very specific about what I like. Even when it came to Pastors I connect to. It has always been very few and far between. God used some amazing worshippers to connect to me and that lead me to a Pastor that delivers messages directly from God's heart to his heart to my ears. One Sunday, Pastor Mike didn't even preach. Worship was on his heart so heavy that it's all the service was, and it was so beautiful. He kept repeating "Worship Is My Weapon," and I understood that from a deep place. That will stay with me forever because it correlates to what Darrel says as well. Instead of focusing on your problems, lift God high in praise. He already knows your problems… but put your trust in him and glorify his name in advance for how he's working it out in your favor. Worship him! The peace that worship has brought me is something I can't even begin to explain in words. But know that I am forever changed.

I was falling so deeply in love with that moment in time. God was getting through to parts of me that I had locked away for so many years. One Sunday in May, Pastor Mike preached "Making Your Pit Your Platform." That message spoke to me so hard. Then, that night during Acts Church, my heart felt particularly heavy. Since it is IG live, I'm usually holding my phone, looking at the screen, locked in. This night, I had my eyes closed as I talked to God while Darrel led us in worship. It's hard to explain, but it felt like a volcano was erupting in my body. And I began having flashbacks of moments in my childhood that I didn't even remember until that moment. It was then that I realized why I couldn't fully heal from certain things; my pain went back further than I thought. But it's as if God wanted me to remember it so I could finally purge it from my heart and let it go. I began to let out a cry that seemed to come from the very pit of my belly, and the tears would not stop. There was no more sound left to come out of my mouth, only tears flowing from my eyes. I took a breath, and at that moment, Darrel said, "He'll mend the broken pieces." Instantly, I knew that was for me. I knew God was talking directly to me. I began to weep on my knees until I could no longer open my eyes. God wanted me to let it go. It was holding me hostage, a prisoner to my own insecurities because of things that happened 30 years ago. I laid on the floor for the next couple of hours, void of all energy but, somehow, I felt lighter than I had felt for as long as I could remember. Those dark corners of my heart that were locked, I felt God invade at that moment, and MAN! It felt GOOD!

From that moment, I began to seek more and more of God. I invited him into my space every day. I talked to him. I adored and loved Him. I praised and thanked Him for the seen and unseen blessings. My relationship with God grew more and more intimate. It was me and Him all day. And there was no place I'd rather be. I honestly can't imagine going back to a place where

God doesn't walk with me every day. I'm so thankful for his friendship. He's such a good father. I didn't know what I was missing in my life. I THOUGHT I knew God already, and yes, I knew of him, but I didn't have a close relationship with him. You don't know what you don't know. All I knew was that God had specific assignments for me, a special purpose for me. What I didn't know was how to unlock what it would be. So, if any of you are feeling a tug of war going on inside of you, understand that God is trying to get your attention. Spend a little time with him, IN A REAL WAY, and watch him reveal some answers you've been searching for.

Although God used the time of quarantine in 2020 to get my attention and get close to Him, this journey of learning who God is, is only just beginning. My desire is to be more of who he designed me to be. Every morning, I ask the Holy Spirit to empty me of me and fill me with more of him. I bring God to me and with me at every moment of my day. I will forever be grateful for how God orchestrated my pull to him. It has been such a beautiful journey thus far and I get excited every moment that I go deeper with him. Acts Church continues to be a necessary part of my walk with the Lord as Darrel continues to be a necessary guide in my growth. I've had the pleasure of meeting him and seeing him worship in person a few times and the anointing on his entire existence is so beautiful to witness. I'm excited to witness how God is moving in his life, and I am so thankful for his life and his obedience. His YES is life-changing for so many people, especially young people, and THAT is what is most beautiful. His gift is multi-dimensional and multi-generational.

Thank you, Darrel for sharing your gift with us. It has forever changed my life.

See you in Acts Church on Sunday!

Chapter 9

My Girl

The moments between December 2020 until Spring 2021 were the most difficult moments in my life. On December 11th, I was at home when I got the call that my mommy passed out getting out of the bathtub. She had been coughing a few days before but we just thought it was a cold. Her doctor prescribed her cough syrup, and we thought nothing more of it. When she fainted getting out of the bathtub, we all agreed she should see a doctor to make sure she didn't injure her head in any way. She didn't injure her head but it turns out the cold was actually Covid. She spent that weekend in the hospital and was released on Monday to finish her quarantine period at home. I called her multiple times a day to check on her. The first couple of days, she sounded a little off on the phone, slurring her words a bit, but not too bad. I just figured it was the medicine she was on. My dad sounded a bit concerned on the phone, stating that she was telling him of conversations with the doctor that he had no knowledge of. I told him I'd come home for a week and check on things. This was Christmas week. When I got home, I was so stunned by her condition. I was in no way prepared for what I was walking into.

If you remember, I told you my mom was a teacher. She taught children at all grade levels for over 30 years. She has helped shape so many children through the Chicago Public School System. Everyone loves her. And let me tell you, as sweet as she is, she is just as much shady! This lady will cut you with her words in the calmest tone and it will literally take you a second to realize she just read you UP AND DOWN! LOL! OMG, she is phenomenal! She has always been the most self-sufficient, independent person I've ever known and what was staring back at me was a fragile, weak, extremely confused lady. Almost unrecognizable from the mom I knew. As I spent a little time with her, I realized that she was extremely delusional and very jittery, and I just couldn't tell on the phone. My brothers had no idea either. I didn't know what I was dealing with, But I was for SURE this was not Covid. I immediately made an appointment with her physician. Since her release from the hospital, she had been assigned a home health nurse. I asked the nurse was this behavior normal for a post-Covid recovery. She said she hadn't seen it before, but a bit of confusion was not uncommon but this is more than confusion. By now, it's been about two weeks since I've been home with my mom, and everyone keeps telling me the same thing; it's just the after-effects of Covid. In my heart of hearts, I knew that just wasn't the case.

For a month straight, it was back and forth with her doctor and back and forth to the ER. Literally, every few days, and it hurt to have to take my mom so often. But just as she held my hand, walking me into the testing center when I was 4 years old, I held her hand each and every time as I sat beside her with these doctors and specialists. The first time I felt she needed to go back to the hospital, she was so disorientated and it scared me SO much! I'll give you a visual. Imagine all the conversations you've had and heard over the last week. Conversations you've had, things you've heard on tv, songs on the radio, things you've overheard other people say. Now I want you to throw ALL those words from all those sentences into a bowl and shake that bowl good to mix them up. Now stick your hand in, pull out 8 or 9 words and put them together to make a sentence. It's almost impossible to make sense because there's so much information in that bowl that's not related. Well, that's how scattered my mom's mind was. And it broke me to my core.

Because the hospitals were so overcrowded due to Covid, they recommended that we call the paramedic and have an ambulance take her. That way she's kept warm and being monitored in the ambulance until a room opens up for her. The first visit, she was in the ambulance for about 3 hours before getting into the hospital. Her vitals were normal, and her oxygen was good, so they saw no need to keep her. They said Covid patients can sometimes experience a period of confusion, so we'd have to just wait it out. I picked her up that night and we went home. She then started complaining of a sharp pain in her stomach and in the upcoming days, her eating got more and more sporadic. She complained that it hurt to swallow and it felt like a sharp block of ice in her throat. It got to where she literally was not eating anything. I started to suspect it may be strep throat, so I called the doctor for a little direction. She called in a prescription for the weekend until we got to the doctor on Monday. (This was a Friday evening) By now, I am a complete wreck on the inside, but of course, I couldn't show any of that. It's like when your child is hurt, as a parent, you put on the strong face and ensure them everything will be ok. You don't want to cause any more panic than there already is, so you bear it alone, so no one else has to. Once again, I've been placed in this position all my life, putting on a happy face while dying on the inside.

On Tuesday we went to see her doctor and she examined her. She tested negative for Strep Throat, but she did develop an infection in her throat. Her doctor and I spoke more about the delusions and disorientation. She made an appointment for mom to have an MRI done the next morning to rule out a stroke. Literally, this is the first time I felt like someone was actually listening to me about how her behavior was not right! I had a brief sigh of relief. Very brief because when we got home, we had to go right back to the ER because there was a chance she had some blood clots forming. My poor baby was so sick of being pricked and poked and transported to the hospital, but we had to go. And by now, she is becoming so child-like in her behavior; it is really breaking my heart. I called 911 and they were on their way. After a few hours, they called and said she could have someone come be with her. They checked her for clotting and didn't find any. Mom was to follow up with her doctor for further testing and they were releasing her. I was over the top, annoyed with everyone at this point. I felt like everyone kept telling us what WASN'T wrong, but no one would tell us what was. Understandably, Covid was taking priority over the medical field, but there is still MORE than Covid out there. I just continued to pray and talk to God, asking him to heal her. You know, I realized some things about how we pray and what we pray while going through all this. I'll get back to that later though.

SO, mommy came home that night and, in the morning, we went to get her MRI. Those results came back negative as well. Again, no answers. I'm gonna run this down for you. My mommy had:

No Stroke

No Strep Throat

No blood clots

Covid symptoms gone

Mass Disorientation

Hallucinations

No ability to eat

Losing the ability to do day to day tasks

Yet, NOT ONE PERSON could give me any explanation for what we were dealing with!

For the next two or so days, mommy's hallucinations and delusions increased. She became really unstable. She kept getting up and sitting back down; she started talking more and more to herself, really erratic. She'd have moments where she'd stare at me and I couldn't see her staring back at me. Forget heartbreaking, my heart had left my chest. By now, we were going on a month being out of the hospital and first being diagnosed with Covid. I wanted to take her back to the hospital that night, but my dad disagreed. He did say if she was like this in the morning, he'd take her himself, so she didn't have to sit in there waiting all night. We monitored her that night and carried on. The next morning, I got up, fixed breakfast, of which she didn't really eat, and I left the house to run some errands.

Remember I told you during all this, I realized some things about how we pray? This is what I meant by that. In my talks and prayer time with God, I would always ask him to heal my mom. "Lord, please heal my mom. God, please take this off of her and heal her." One day out of nowhere, it popped in my head that maybe my healing for her doesn't look like the Lord's healing for her. I sat with that for a minute. I knew God wanted me to get something out of that, but he was going to make me figure that one out on my own. I just began praying for her again, and I started weeping. "Lord heal my mommy. Make her better." I dropped to my knees and just thanked him for whatever he had coming. And then it hit me. MY healing for her that I was asking for was for her to go back to the mommy I'd always known her to be. But what if God had other plans.

Cue Rich Tolbert Jr:

"God knows the plans he has for me. He knows the thoughts he thinks towards me. And NOTHING is an accident, I'M ALIVE because there's more."

Instantly, I shifted my posture and began to pray for the Lord to heal her "HOWEVER THAT LOOKED TO HIM!" Even my language changed. Because it's not enough to just say something that sounds good, you have to believe what you are saying. I begin to talk to God about this. I told him I understood now. I thanked him for saving her life. And I believed him to be a healer and a miracle worker; whatever healing looked like to him, I welcomed it with trust and gratitude. My dialogue with other people changed the same way. People would say, "I'm praying for your mom; she will be better." My response became, "His will, his way. Whatever healing looks like to the Lord, I welcome it." I'm sure no one understood why I began saying that, but the thing is, I was still holding on to MY plans for her healing. That meant I wasn't fully trusting him. As if he wasn't in total control anyway! I didn't have control over this. HE DID! But I realized I wasn't fully committed to believing that. Once I shifted my posture and my mind frame, that's when he delivered her healing. Don't get me wrong, her being sick wasn't about me, but like Darrel says, "What he allows, he uses," and God was definitely showing me he was God.

Now I want you to pay attention because this part is going to go fast. Buckle up.

I was out running errands and my dad calls me. He says my mom wants to go back to the hospital when she has never WANTED to go. I told Him to take her and I'd meet them there. We were not going to stall when her own mind told her to go back. When I arrived, she was at the desk checking in. The nurse said to go to the waiting room and wait for triage to come get her. Now, I just KNEW the room was going to be packed; we would probably be standing. This was my thought as we walked across the hall. Do you want to know how many people were waiting in the room when we turned the corner? Come on, guess!! Ok, I'll tell you. ZERO! NOT ONE SOUL was in that waiting room! I was shocked. I still didn't get the full picture; hold on, I know you don't either. So, we were waiting about 5 minutes when triage came to get us, and the triage nurse was so sweet and genuinely concerned. I began to tell her my mom's symptoms and after a few, she cut me off; "Oh goodness baby, that's enough! I got you. We're gonna get her taken care of!" She called to the back and asked about open rooms. She told me to have another seat in the waiting room and they would come and get us shortly. We were there maybe another 3 minutes and she came and got us herself and walked us back to the back to a room. As soon as I got my mom seated on the bed, the doctor walks in. NOT THE NURSE, but the doctor himself! We talked for a second and then he asked her a few questions to see how coherent she was. He also seemed genuinely concerned, and I started to feel a little lighter. He told me he wanted to do another CAT Scan and we would go from there. So, we sat about 10 minutes, the nurse came in, took some blood, started a drip… you know, nurse things. Then they came and did a chest x-ray and within another 20 minutes came to get her for the cat scan. About 20 minutes later, they brought her back and there was another person who came with her. He was the intake counselor for the Behavioral Health center. He informed they were going to admit her to get her tested and treated for dementia. I instantly just started crying in relief! THIS IS ALL I HAD BEEN WANTING!!! Someone to see what I saw, that this was NOT Covid and something was wrong! I sat with her until they took her to the center across the street and then I went home. Mind you; I didn't see the initial doctor other than the one time when we first arrived.

It took about 5 minutes in my car for my mind to process all that had just happened in the last hour and a half. And I began to cry out to God like never before and thanked him for being Sovereign and faithful. You see, GOD set those pieces up perfectly. I hadn't said ANYTHING different that I hadn't been saying for the last month. I never took my foot off the gas with how hard I went for these doctors to pay attention to her. But THIS time, they did. God put it in HER mouth that this was the moment she needed to go to the ER. There was NO ONE waiting. NO ONE!! The triage nurse got us to the back almost instantly and the doctor himself was the FIRST person to come in. Usually, it's the nurse. It was the doctor. Then he never came back to talk to me or anything. GOD DID THAT! Listen! I need you to understand this in real time. For a month, these ER visits have been LONG. She'd spend 3 hours in the ambulance before she made it inside. But this time, we got in, got treated, had CAT scans and x-rays, and she was processed and admitted to a different facility in UNDER the time she had been waiting to get inside before. You can NOT tell me God is not good!

I really could not stop crying. It's truly something when you witness firsthand how he moves. So now I had to let them do their thing. She was in the hospital for a little more than a week. Close to two. They got her set on a medication that keeps her stable during the day and one that helped her sleep at night. Does she still have moments of confusion? Of course, she does. Dementia is not something that goes away. And it will progress over time. But I got what I prayed for, her healing. Like I said, so many people have lost their lives to Covid-19 and those numbers continue to rise at this moment. God saw fit that my mommy wasn't one of them. I hated her suffering. Can you imagine being locked inside your mind all day and not being able to formulate a thought that makes sense? Me either, but I've seen it up close now, and it breaks you down to your core to see your loved one going through it. When I started trusting God for healing on HIS terms, the healing came.

Once again, I don't know God's plans… but in this season, I

have learned to submit and release control fully to Him. I am so grateful for His friendship… for His faithfulness, and His never-ending love. It is truly amazing to think that God will never love us any more OR less than he does right now because His love for us is perfect at ALL TIMES!

"For I know the plans I have for you. They are plans to prosper you and not to harm you. Plans to give you hope and a future."

Jeremiah 29:11

Chapter 10

Make The Exchange

God is in every little detail of your day… every detail of your week… every detail of your year. God is with you in every detail of your entire life. What we must do is learn to be sensitive to his voice. I am just now at the beginning of this new chapter of my life, so while you learn of my past in these pages, I'm asking God to guide the very specific path to my future. I never imagined that God would use me in the ways he has thus far, so I can't even begin to envision how He will use me in the days to come. But what I know is this: my life matters. My life has purpose. My life is a gift. My life is intentional. God knew what He was doing when He created me. He knew how He wanted to use me to get His glory. He foresaw all the mistakes I'd make… all the roads that would lead to heartbreak and confusion. He saw all the tears. And He designed my life to include all of that, knowing He would carry me through it all. He had a plan to heal me from all of it; all I had to do was turn to Him and stop running away from Him.

My life has been a journey. These pages only give you a glimpse, and if the Lord allows, I'll have decades more to continue to learn and grow in my walk with Christ. The things I've gone through and witnessed have given me a lot of wisdom. I pray that as you read some of my most private feelings, thoughts and life moments, you'll understand life the way I now see it. It took the things I've gone through, the experiences I've had and the lessons I've learned in order for me to see God in all His glory through these lenses. I once saw a video of a child who was born with a hearing defect who had just got implants and heard his mother's voice for the first time. He didn't know what sound was, so he adapted to life without it. But that first time the switch was turned on and he heard his mother's voice was the most beautiful and humbling sight. The one who brings him peace when he's anxious; comfort when he's afraid. The one who provides food when he's hungry and rocks him to sleep, safely in her arms. The one who he relies on for everything now has a unique sound attached to her. The way that little boy's face lit up and how emotional he got brought me to tears! That's how I feel every day. I didn't know what being in true relationship with God was really like. Even the years I THOUGHT I knew God turned out to only be me knowing Of Him. The feeling I have in my heart every day is one I never want to lose. Once I gave God permission to come into my life and have His way, He freed and healed me. I gave my life completely to Him and it's been the sweetest love I've ever known.

My DAILY prayer is for God to empty me of me and fill me with more of Him so that when people look at me, ALL they see is him; and to please never leave me because I never want to not feel this way. I have such a long way to go, but it's not a sprint. Progression, Not Perfection. That's the goal.

There are a few things I want you to take away from my journey. Ready?

God is Sovereign.

God reigns with ALL POWER. There is nothing too hard, too complicated or too ugly for God because He created all thing and knows all things. Don't ever think you're hiding anything from Him. He sees everything. I saw an interview once where the guy said the reason why God isn't here in the universe is because He's the creator OF the universe; so in order for Him to create it, he has to be outside of it. My jaw dropped; I promise. Profound statements such as that leave an imprint on me and have me deep in thought. He's right. God created the heavens and the Earth. How could He be inside of it? But He knew we would need Him because we're flawed, not perfect like him, so what did He do? He sent Jesus to be a savior for our sins that we'd undoubtedly have, and then because He knew we'd need daily help, He gave us Holy Spirit to be our help and guide for the rest of our days. If you truly believe that in your heart, then you'll see God's face one day. Simple. I say simple, but it's not a simple concept for some, I know. People need proof to believe when all we need to do is believe and God will make your life the proof! WHEW! (That was GOOD, Keke!) It's so true though! God will make miracle after miracle after show up in your life when you believe with the expectation that He will. Fear has no chance up against God; God silences fear. He calms your storms. He just wants your YES.

God doesn't need your permission to be God.

If there is a calling on your life, nothing you can do will hinder that. The anointing is on YOU, not your actions. We have free will, so we can decide what we do. However, with even you making a decision, God will decide how that decision will play out. He's always in control, please don't ever forget that. Often, we get so anxious about how something is going to turn out, all because we don't see movement happening when WE want it to happen. God doesn't work on our timeline; we exist on his. If we relinquish control, the control that we don't even have, may I add, and wait on God to do what He does, we'd be so stress-free walking through life. I know, I know. Waiting on provision or answers we aren't sure is going to come is hard. But that's where your faith has to overpower your fear. Darrel always says, "God ain't raise no punk Christians," and although I think that is just the most hilarious thing when he says it. I had to think about that statement for what it is. The enemy is working overtime to destroy. He is using culture, the media and the internet to cause chaos and corrupt our children, filling their time and thoughts with everything but God. He is also working overtime to destroy the sanctity of marriage and families, leaving children searching for answers in everything but God. (Please remember these are MY opinions and observations) This generation has to be stronger than ever and more planted than ever before in the word of God. We have to be sensitive to God's voice to know when it's him leading us and not the enemy tricking us. Our posture has to be total submission. God wants to bless us abundantly. I have a habit of saying, “I don’t reward bad behavior.” That made me think; God doesn’t reward bad behavior either. Turn to him, then wait. Wait on him to show up and show out! God is still in the business of miracles. What makes you think he doesn’t have some for you? God is our Father, and our Father is the King. What King wouldn’t want his children living well? Patience in waiting stirs strength inside of you that you didn’t know you had. And, while you wait for God to work his plans, just worship. Thank him for what He’s doing because you know whatever it is, it’s going to work in your favor. If you don’t know how, just make worship intentional in your life until it becomes a natural part of your life. I promise it gets easier.

Before you were born, God had a plan for you, one that’s still intact today.

God decided what you would look like, what your personality would be, what your purpose would be and what you needed in your life to fulfill that. He was very intentional with you. Sometimes, if we find ourselves in a less than favorable situation, we automatically think we’re somehow less than or not loved as much or even at all. We ask ourselves if God loves us, how could he allow us to be in so much pain? Or how could he allow so many bad things to happen? It’s like I said, we have choices in life, and yes, God chooses what he allows. But WHAT HE ALLOWS, HE USES. Bad things are going to happen. God never said they wouldn't. What he DID say was that he would be there to sustain you in the middle of your storm. He promised to be your anchor in the middle of the storm so you would not drift off the course he set you on. He promised he'd be your guide if you only allow him to take the reins and take your hands off of everything. God didn't say the storms wouldn't come, but hc promised that the storm wouldn't drown you as long as he was with you. So, the question I want you to ask yourself is if God is truly with you? Do you trust him? When your season has been dark for so long that you can't see any possible end, can you still look to God with all faith and say, "God I trust whatever you're doing"? It's completely ok to tell God, "I have no clue what you're doing or why!" as long as at the end of that, you say, "But I trust you." God is not afraid of your questions. He wants you to come to him with all of your concerns, all of your questions, all of your doubts, your fears… even your heartaches. God wants to sit with you in your sadness and help you heal. He hates to see us hurt and not coming to him for help. Remember, He's our Father; a loving, kind and patient Father. He wants to help. He wants to give us answers for our questions. He wants to give us healing for our hurt. We have to set our pride aside and ask him for help. It may not seem like it, but everything is working for your good. All the pieces are aligning for YOUR good; and God is setting up your miracles to get HIS glory. And let me tell you something; YOU ARE THE MIRACLE! Your life is a miracle! He chose every detail about you that makes you who you are!

OF COURSE, he wants the absolute best for you!

You were born for this moment in time.

Your assignment is not for 30 years ago. It's not for 30 years from now. It's for RIGHT NOW! Yes, you have an assignment and it's waiting on you to complete it right now. Who you are is born for a time such as this. Your past doesn't disqualify you; it prepares you. What you have on the inside of you is meant for today. Your thoughts, your dreams, your hopes and your heart… all meant for right now. We are here on this earth not for ourselves but for others that God knows only we can reach with the gifts He's placed inside us. As I said, the calling is on you, not your actions. God will NEVER love you any more or any less than He does at this very moment. His love is perfect at all times and never changing. There's nothing you could ever do to separate yourself from the love of God. It's His breathe in our lungs… He put the beat in our hearts. Him. Our father! He loves us and only wants the best for us. It's only fear or lack of knowledge that will have you believe that God will abandon His love for you because you messed up or disappointed Him. When He created us, He factored in all of our mistakes. His glory lives on the other side of those mistakes. I've made so many mistakes in my life. I'm not perfect by a long shot, and I still make mistakes. I'm growing every day. That's all I can hope for. We will never be perfect. All we can hope is that every day that the Lord allows us to exist, we do a little better than the day before… that we're a little more aware of His presence and we acknowledge and honor Him more.

Finally, what I want you to take away is this:

Trust requires total faith, just as faith requires total trust.

Putting your trust in the unknown and unseen, I know, can be scary, especially if you believe you haven't seen God show up for you in a way that's visibly clear. Believe me when I say that God has been fighting battles for you since the very first day of your creation. He's protected you from storms both seen and unseen and he's guided you even when you didn't know it. That little nudge in the pit of your stomach, anytime you've said "I had a feeling" or "Something told me," that was Holy Spirit helping to guide you. But to truly trust God, you have to have complete and blind faith that He is going to work it out for you because He will. Again, it's ok to have some questions for God. You can talk to Him and say, "Hey God, I feel like nothing's going right in my life right now. I feel like every time I take a step forward, I get knocked 8 steps back." It's ok to tell your Father, "Lord, I'm losing all my faith right now. My soul feels weakened. I need your help." I can't count how many times I have gone to God on my knees weeping, scared because it seemed my dark season was never going to end. I use to beg God to fix it, take it away… make it better. Now, when I go to God in a time of sorrow, it sounds more like, "Lord you good. You are perfect. I know you are working on my behalf, and your glory will be beautiful. But right now, God, my core is a little shaken. Please send healing for my soul and peace for my heart because I know you got me; my flesh is just taking over my spirit right now because I'm scared." Can you imagine how many of these conversations I went to God with while my mom was sick? This was when God took the opportunity to teach me that in my darkest time, He would stay beside me, that He would NEVER leave me, as long as I trust him. On the other side of that trust is faith. Textbook definition of faith is confidence in what we hope for and the assurance that the Lord is working, even though we cannot see it. Confidence. That's a big word that packs a lot of emotions. When you've been hurt or disappointed, frustrated or let down, it's hard to have confidence that some things are working in your favor. We tend to cast our earthly fears and feelings on a supernatural God, and that's just not how that works. We can't take our hurt and pain out on God for something someone did to us or made us feel. Make trusting God a conscience part of your day until it becomes an effortless part of your heart.

While I was going through my storms, the abuse, the disappointment, the abandonment and the trauma, I didn't have my eyes on God, and because I didn't, I couldn't see that He always had His hands on me. From the very beginning, God had a plan for me. He designed me so intentionally. I don't know how my story ends… I'm only just beginning to scratch the surface. But what I know for certain is that God will guide me through every moment. He will always be there to comfort me during the rough times, just as he will always be there to magnify my good times. In both instances, God's glory will reside, and I take so much comfort in that. This life is hard. My heart is so sensitive. The safe space in worship and relationship with God is something I longed for my entire life. It's something I knew I craved, but I began to think didn't exist because of how my love had been mishandled all my life. Love. Real, pure, genuine LOVE. Love that has no restrictions. Love that knows no boundaries. When I am in God's presence, I am an open door. I give Him all authority to shine a light on every corner of my heart, my mind and my soul. All that I am, all that I have, belongs to Him. I will never take this beautiful gift called life for granted. When I wasn't even looking for Him, God was looking for me. He healed my whole heart in ways I didn't even know were broken. I made the exchange with Him, and he gave me Beauty For Ashes. I pray you find your healing. I pray you trust the safety that lies in the arms of our Father. I pray you make the exchange.

Made in the USA
Monee, IL
10 September 2026

62770619R00075